Winning Through

I CAN'T FACE TOMORROW

Considers what makes people suicidal, how to recognize
the warning signs of an impending attempt, the effects of
suicide on those who are left, our attitude to suicide, and
most importantly, what family, friends and colleagues can
do to help the potential suicide.

Winning Through

I CAN'T FACE
TOMORROW

*Help for Those with Thoughts of
Suicide and Those who Counsel Them*

NORMAN KEIR

THORSONS PUBLISHING GROUP

First published 1986

© NORMAN KEIR 1986

British Library Cataloguing in Publication Data

Keir, Norman
I can't face tomorrow: help for those troubled
by thoughts of suicide.
1. Suicide — Prevention
I. Title
362.2'0425   HV6545

ISBN 0-7225-1256-2

*Published by Thorsons Publishers Limited,
Wellingborough, Northamptonshire, NN8 2RQ, England*

Printed in Great Britain by Biddles Limited, Guildford, Surrey

3   5   7   9   10   8   6   4   2

CONTENTS

ACKNOWLEDGEMENTS

'All that we are', The Dhammapada says, 'is the result of what we have thought; it is founded on our thoughts and made up of our thoughts.' I believe this to be true and I recognize, therefore, that many people have played a part in making me the kind of person that I now am; they share with me the blame and, if any is due, the credit for Norman Keir. They have thus contributed indirectly to the provision of much that has gone into this book. They cannot, however, be held responsible for its shortcomings; the blame for these is mine and mine alone, for it is I who have made the synthesis. The same is true of those who have given me direct assistance, and whose help I gladly acknowledge. In doing so I wish to be absolved from having to place their names in any suggestive sequence. I shall therefore take refuge in alphabetical order, which favours none.

So first I wish to thank Pat Anderson, a friend of three decades; it was he who first got me involved in trying to help the suicidal. Then I must thank Dr Jim Birley for encouraging me to think that I might be able to produce something of value to the general reader. He also drew my attention to some useful references, as did Fred Clements and John Coggrave. The Reverend David Evans gave me a great deal of help in tracking down information, and Simon Franklin of Thorsons Publishing Group has made it all much easier than I could ever have anticipated. Dr Bob Good made me stop and think about the possibility of finding examples of suicidal thought in literature. David Henderson brought a useful book across the Atlantic and Jean Machell took over the task of finding most of the other books I needed. Tony Milne taught me all I know about counselling and also suggested some useful sources of information. Dr Keith Norcross spotted a useful paper in a medical journal to which I would not otherwise have had access. Last but by no means least I must thank my wife, who, since her name is Audrey, might logically have headed this list. Indeed she should have, for along with my mother and daughter, she has been available when I needed her and discreetly absent when I wished to be left to work alone. Many errors which might have joined those which may remain were removed at her suggestion.

FOREWORD

The man who, in a fit of melancholy, kills himself today, would have wished to live had he waited a week.

Voltaire

'I'm going to kill myself.'

'What's wrong?'

'Everything. Everybody. Me.'

'Tell me.'

'You wouldn't want to hear it.'

'Tell me about today. What happened today?'

'They had a meeting. I think it all came out. I'll lose my job, of course. I'll lose everything.'

'Your family?'

'I can't face what this will do to them.'

'If you . . . how would you kill yourself?'

'Simple. I've got a gun.'

'Where is it?'

'Here. On the table.'

'Is anyone else there?'

'They've all gone for the weekend.'

'Could you put the gun away, while we talk? Time. Give yourself some time. Put the gun where you can't see it.'

'I want it under my hand. I've got to get out of this. I've got to escape.'

A Samaritan volunteer, taking a call like that, has to hang on to the hope that even in such a crisis, this man does not totally wish to die. He wants to kill himself to escape the intolerable emotional pain, but he does not want to be dead for ever. That's why he made the call. That's why it can be possible to help even the acutely suicidal person to save his own life.

Suicide is not just the business of therapists and counsellors and groups like The Samaritans. It is everybody's business, and it's a growing tragedy none of us can ignore. In the words that Arthur Miller gave to Willie Loman's wife in *Death of a Salesman*, 'Attention must be paid'.

Norman Keir's book is tremendously important in bringing the hidden and secret subject of suicide out into the open, to lead us towards understanding, so that we may help other people — and ourselves. There is no 'Us' and 'Them'. Suicidal people are not insane. They are you and me, given unendurable circumstances.

After a suicide, you may hear, 'We never thought . . . if only we'd known . . .', but later it's remembered that there were clues and signs of desperation to which nobody paid attention. The person may even have said, 'I wish I was dead', without anyone daring to follow it up with, 'Do you really mean that?'

If you are seriously worried about someone, the most helpful thing you can do is to ask, in your own words, 'Is it bad enough to make you think about killing yourself?'

Afraid that might put the idea into their head? You couldn't, if it wasn't there already, which it may well be. Afraid of opening a can of worms? But how are you going to help if you're not willing to hear the very worst of it? Afraid you won't know what to say? But it's not you who is going to be doing the saying. It's the unhappy person. You'll be listening.

Whatever the individual reasons for suicide, there are always large elements of loss, compounded into that one real killer — loss of self-esteem. So the aim of the response is to try in any way possible to help the suffering person to feel better about themselves. Showing your own liking is important, and it's a natural instinct to like someone who turns to you for help. 'I care whether you live or die.' That's a start, at least.

Imagine a terrible circumstance that could make you feel like killing yourself. What would help? What would not help?

I know that I would *not* want someone who would: change the subject, try to make me cheer up and count my blessings, give me a lecture, preach, be shocked or afraid of me, make me feel guilty (I'd feel that already), offer love insincerely, tell me their own troubles — or those of their cousin's sister-in-law, dole out clichés, instantly recommend a psychiatrist, look at their watch . . .

The things I *would* want are few and plain, from someone who would: take me seriously, keep quiet and listen, value my life.

Simple, isn't it? No mystique about it. Nothing there that anyone could not provide, whether you are a professional, or an ordinary person who wants to help.

If someone comes to you in critical distress, don't be afraid of your own inadequacy. You have what's needed, if you have a pair of ears and the patience to use them creatively, and for as long as it takes.

Don't be afraid of the responsibility. The other person's life or death is their own responsibility. You can't save a life. But you may be fortunate enough to be given the chance to support someone in saving their own life.

If you are interested in this book because you are agonisingly familiar yourself with thoughts of suicide, please don't be afraid to tell someone. Asking for help is not a weakness. It's a strength you can be proud of. Give yourself every possible chance. If you find yourself overwhelmed by the impulse to take your life, give yourself a bit more time. Consider, with Voltaire, that it had better wait a while. After all, you could still kill yourself tomorrow, or the day after, or next week . . . if you still want to.

MONICA DICKENS

Dedicated to The Samaritans

INTRODUCTION

This book is about suicide. The subject is one which, directly or indirectly, affects many lives. Each year a significant number of people kill themselves or are bereaved by suicide. Many more contemplate or unsuccessfully attempt self-destructive action. There can be few who have not known, or known of, someone who has died by his own hand. Suicide is the cause — and the result — of much misery. It is a subject, therefore, about which we should be well-informed; we should know what causes it and what may be done to avert it. Sadly, however, most of us know very little, and misconceptions abound. One reason for our lack of knowledge is that 'suicide, even publicly committed, remains the most private and impenetrable of human acts.'[1] We may receive hints that a person has suicidal intent but we are unlikely to be privy to all his thoughts, and what is left behind after the act has been committed seldom provides much enlightenment.

There is another reason for our ignorance: we do not, in truth, really want to know. Of all human actions there is none we find more disturbing than suicide. However often we have encountered it, each fresh occurrence leaves us with a feeling of unease. Those of us who are disposed to be optimistic, welcoming each new day, or even just most days, as a challenge or a pleasure, find it difficult to conceive of the thought processes that might have led someone to take his own life. We might have been able to consider in a purely hypothetical way the circumstances that could lead us to suicide, but to grasp how the victim must have felt is beyond us. 'What could have driven him to do such a thing?' is the question which most commonly occupies our minds when we hear that an acquaintance has killed himself. Contemplation of the deed itself, the manner of its execution — the overdose, the drowning, the hanging — fills us with horror. Our imagination

falters when we try to create in our minds the thoughts and
feelings the victim might have had as he initiated the fatal act.
Why do we react in this way? After all, are we not exposed through
television and the other media to the whole spectrum of human
suffering and tragedy? Admittedly death in any form seems
virtually to occupy the place held by sex in Victorian society:
it is something we would rather not discuss, almost as if we wished
to pretend it did not exist. But suicide, perhaps even more than
any other subject, arouses embarrassment when it is permitted
entry into our conversation. Hearing that I was about to embark
on the writing of this book, a friend asked me what it was to
be about. When I told him, his discomfort was almost palpable
and the subject was hastily dropped. Reflecting on this, I realized
that the embarrassment had started with me. I would rather he
had not asked me, for I had been aware that we would be opening
a door he would in all probability have preferred to leave closed.
We may feel moderately comfortable about discussing suicide
in a general and theoretical way, but when we get down to cases
or when we are in company where intimate, personal conversation
is the norm it is not a welcome topic. The reason is perhaps that,
in talking about our feelings on suicide, we should inevitably be
risking entry into an area where strong emotions reside. This,
however, must be only part of the story, for many counsellors
well accustomed to dealing with strong emotions would confess
to having felt uncomfortable when the subject of suicide has
arisen. Asked why, they might proffer a variety of reasons, but
behind them all is probably the fact that when we speak of suicide
we are probing close to the mainspring of life: the will to live.
Albert Camus put it succinctly:

> There is but one truly serious philosophical problem, and that
> is suicide. Judging whether life is or is not worth living amounts
> to answering the fundamental question of philosophy.[2]

Hence there is widespread what he so aptly calls 'an absurd
sensitivity' on the subject.

Later we shall have more to say about attitudes towards suicide,
but for the present let us think for a moment why anyone should
wish to read about a subject which for many people comes close
to being regarded as taboo. Well — let's be honest — taboos are
interesting, but the satisfaction of mere morbid curiosity is no
justification for setting out to produce the serious account of the
subject this volume is intended to be. It is here that the reader

has an advantage over the author. With the book in his hand and having quickly run an eye over the list of contents the reader already knows more about the author and the purpose of his book than can be known of the reader's needs when writing commences. So certain assumptions have to be made. Three groups of readers have been envisaged. First there is the general reader who wishes to know more about the behaviour of his fellow men (and, for once and for all, please accept that this is intended to include her and her fellow women). Among this group may be those whose non-professional activities, such as counselling, bring them into contact with the suicidal or their families. It may also include professional workers who wish to have a convenient assemblage of information on the subject.

A second group of readers may be those who have been plagued by thoughts of suicide or have been frightened by suicidal urges. They will wish to know that they are not in some way abnormal, that it *is* possible for someone else to have some kind of understanding of how they feel and that they can find help if they want it. They may find it of some reassurance to know that, though discussion of suicide may for the reasons referred to above be uncommon, suicidal thoughts and impulses are not.

Finally there will be some who have been distressed to have heard about the self-destruction of a friend or of some celebrity and who feel it would help to think through the event and the emotions it has aroused in them. Perhaps those most in need of support are the family, friends and colleagues of someone who has died by his own hand. They may be the unintended victims of the act, suffering a bereavement which was its by-product rather than its purpose, or they may indeed be the persons towards whom the suicide's anger, turned against himself though it was, originally was directed. Theirs is a difficult but not insuperable task: to overcome the feelings of guilt the act has generated and to try to understand the motives which led to it.

With the object of responding to the needs of these three groups of readers the book has been designed as a general survey of all the main aspects of the subject. Thus it sets out to present the facts about suicide and its prevalence, and to examine the possible causes, including depression and bereavement. In looking at causes it draws on studies of suicide in literature — such as Tolstoy's *Anna Karenina* and Flaubert's *Madame Bovary*. On a very practical level, it seeks to draw the reader's attention to those signs which might alert him to the danger of suicide in those around him. There is also a chapter on parasuicide and on the effect this act and suicide itself have on those who have been close to the victim. Attitudes to suicide are discussed, including the views of those who regard it, or have in the past regarded it, with approval or disapproval and consideration is given to how one might arrive at a personal decision on the morality of suicide. The question of prevention is also addressed, and the work of the Samaritans is discussed. The book ends with some suggestions for further reading.

One of the problems of exploring the subject of suicide is, as has already been mentioned, the impossibility of arriving at a complete and true understanding of the state of mind of those who take their own lives. For this reason, if for no other, I have relied upon the perceptions of poets and novelists rather than upon actual case studies. I believe that a Shakespeare or a Tolstoy can bring us closer to the truth than the victim himself can. But there is another reason. The many suicidal people to whom I have listened have spoken of their thoughts and feelings on the clear understanding that what they have said will go no further. That is a trust which can never be betrayed.

The reader might quite understandably wish to establish the perspective from which the book has been written. Just as one likes to know the political persuasion of the main speaker before deciding whether to attend an election meeting so one might reasonably wish to know where the author stands on the subject of the book one is about to read. I do have thoughts and feelings about suicide but I feel that it is important to be dispassionate on the matter. So I crave the reader's indulgence in allowing me to stand aloof, at least until a postscript. For the present let it suffice to say that for me what matters most about suicide is that the victim goes through a period of suffering which in the end becomes intolerable. If we are to help the suicidal person we have to support him in his efforts to deal constructively with the life he finds less acceptable than extinction. If we are to do anything for those who are bereaved we have to help them in their efforts to cope with a life which will always include the absence of someone who has in the past been an integral part of it. Somehow they both must learn how to cope — and suicide is not coping. They must have help to discover how to face tomorrow.

1.

THE FACTS

The Doctor said that death was but a scientific fact.

Oscar Wilde, *The Ballad of Reading Gaol*

It seems sensible to start with what we know about suicide, the facts about its occurrence and so on. There are, however, many pitfalls and it soon becomes apparent that much of what we might at first sight regard as factual is highly suspect. Scientists searching for experimental data are familiar with the problem. As one distinguished physicist, Werner Heisenberg, put it, 'What we observe is not nature itself, but nature exposed to our method of questioning.'[3] The measurements we make, our very observations, are dependent upon the methods we use. Thus, if we were to ask a suicidal person why he felt the way he did, the answer we received would depend at least to some extent upon how our question had been framed. Even the suicide note has to be interpreted with care, because the victim tells us only what he wants us to know.

Similar reservations apply to suicide statistics. The verisimilitude that the presentation of numerical information lends to a thesis is often spurious. The argument that graphs seem to support may be false. We must question the validity of any data produced. Have they been collected by reliable and consistent means? Has the information we use in comparing the behaviours of two populations been gathered in the same way? In other words are we comparing like with like? When we examine the figures derived from a sample of the population we have to be certain that the sample is representative. When we have established that a trend exists we have to remember that any assertion about its continuation into the future is an act of faith. When we detect that two trends are parallel we have to be wary of assuming that they are related, and before we can say that any such relationship implies an actual interaction or a common underlying cause a great deal of corroborative work has to be done. The point is entertainingly made in the following quotation given in *The Frank Muir Book*:[4]

> Since tea has been in fashion, even *suicide* has been more familiar among us than in times past.
>
> Jonas Hanway (1712-86), 'An Essay on Tea'*

If we are to take Mr Hanway seriously we must be aware that he has committed two sins. Not only has he implied a causal relationship between two probably unrelated trends, but it seems that he has also selected the data to support his argument. Perhaps elsewhere in his essay he justifies such a procedure, like the lawyer who is alleged to have addressed the jury with the words, 'The following are the conclusions on which I have based my facts.' Amusing, maybe, but such procedures can creep into serious argument inadvertently or even otherwise.

The relevance of this preamble becomes evident as soon as we begin to examine the statistics that are available on suicide. It is often extremely difficult or even impossible to discover whether suicide has taken place. If death has been by hanging, the verdict can be reasonably certain, provided foul play can be eliminated. When death has resulted from an overdose of drugs the possibility of accident cannot always be excluded. In the case of death by drowning, suicide may be suspected but it is usually hard to prove. It is the law in this country that suicide must never be presumed to be the cause of death merely because it appears to be the most likely explanation; evidence is required. Two other factors militate against the recording of suicide as the cause of death. The first is the community attitude towards suicide. Where the general feeling is that self-destruction is sinful or a matter for shame, coroners are often reluctant to bring in a verdict of suicide.

---

* George Borrow (*Lavengro*, J. M. Dent, 1924) suggested that there was a possible connection between the fact that the Germans 'are the greatest smokers' and the observation that suicide 'is not a national habit in Germany, as it is in England'.

The other factor is the coroner himself. Some coroners are less
disposed than others to accept suicide as the cause of death. It
has been said that one medical examiner in the British Isles has
never recorded a verdict of suicide in his whole life. As recently
as November 1985[5] it was reported that a decision by the High
Court of Dublin earlier in the year had meant that verdicts of
suicide could no longer be brought in by coroners in the Republic
of Ireland. The law preventing coroners from apportioning blame
has been extended to prohibit them from blaming victims for
their own deaths.

When comparisons are being made between countries, account
has to be taken not only of varying attitudes but of different
procedures adopted in recording cause of death. In some
countries the fact that suicide has taken place is noted at the
registry office when the death is registered and in some, but not
all, cases the suicide is recorded on the actual register. It may be
that the registrar asks the cause of death and passes the information
on to a central office where statistics are recorded. Elsewhere the
cause of death is shown on the documents of official proceedings,
which may be to do with the police or the medical authorities
or both. In some countries the responsibility for ascertaining the
cause of death rests with the judicial administration. Moreover,
in some countries suicide may be presumed in the absence of
evidence to the contrary.

One conclusion to be drawn is that only a fraction of all suicides
are recorded and any statement about how large the fraction is
must contain a considerable element of guesswork. A second
conclusion is that the fraction of suicides that are recorded almost
certainly varies from country to country, from population to
population. It might be added that it is not only the authorities
responsible for recording suicide and the procedures they employ
that contribute to the inaccuracy of the figures. Sometimes those
who take their own lives attempt to conceal the suicidal nature
of their deaths in order to spare their families from the additional
pain this kind of bereavement causes. They do so by contriving
to make their death seem to have resulted from an accident. Thus
no one can estimate just how many unexplained road accidents
have been deliberate.

Another, perhaps less obvious problem arises when we deal with
the question of suicide: what do we mean by the word? There
is a wide spectrum of acts and patterns of behaviour to which

the term *suicidal* might reasonably be attached. The renowned French sociologist, Emile Durkheim, to whose book, *Le Suicide*,[6] first published in 1897, we shall make reference in subsequent chapters, offered the following definition:

> ... the term *suicide* is applied to all cases of death resulting directly or indirectly from a positive or negative act of the victim himself, which he knows will produce this result.

This definition includes not only positive acts of self-destruction, such as cutting or the ingestion of lethal doses of drugs, but also intentionally fatal negative acts, such as the refusal to take food. Also covered is the action of the person whose death is intended to achieve martyrdom or the heroic deed of a soldier, which he knows will bring about his death. Durkheim's definition makes no differentiation between an action which has death as its sole purpose and the action of the hero, whose aim is to save his platoon and whose death is an unavoidable incidental. It would exclude, however, all self-inflicted deaths where the victim is unaware of the necessary consequence of his act. Thus Durkheim excludes death that results from hallucination, for example when someone jumps out of an upper window believing it to be on the ground floor. He also excludes self-destructive acts by animals, which in his estimation do not have the understanding necessary to anticipate their deaths. The key to Durkheim's definition is that at the moment he commits the act that is destined to be fatal the victim knows the normal result of it with certainty. 'Introduce a few doubts,' says Durkheim, 'and you have a new act, not suicide but closely akin to it, since only a difference of degree exists between them.'

One of Durkheim's early followers was Maurice Halbwachs, whose book, *Les Causes du Suicide*,[7] was published in 1930. Halbwachs felt that it was not enough to give a purely scientific definition of suicide as Durkheim had done. He thought that it was necessary to take account of the attitude of society. He cites two examples. The first is the person who through gluttony or intemperance refuses to follow a moderate diet which he knows to be the only way to postpone his death. The second is the one referred to by Durkheim, the soldier who courts death to save his friends. Both would be included in Durkheim's definition of suicide, which does not differentiate between acts in which it has been accepted that death is only a necessary condition to which one must submit in order to attain a certain desire and those where death has been sought for its own sake. In Halbwachs' view society would not regard the two examples quoted as being instances of suicide. 'It is . . . not proper', he says, 'to call suicide the Christian act of a martyr who, knowing he will be punished by death, undertakes to overthrow idols.' He suggests modifying Durkheim's definition to 'all cases of death resulting from an act accomplished by the victim himself with the intention or the view to killing himself'. He considers adding the rider, 'and which is not demanded or approved by society', but he recognizes that there *are* suicides that are demanded by society, for example the practice of *suttee* in which widows in India were at one time expected to immolate themselves on their husbands' funeral pyres. Another rider he considers is 'and which does not have an altruistic aim', but this would exclude all those suicides where one departs from life in order not to be a burden to one's family. Halbwachs finally arrives at the following:

> We classify as suicide every case of death which results from an act accomplished by the victim himself with the intention or with a view to killing himself, and which is not a sacrifice.[7]

By *sacrifice* Halbwachs has in mind the soldier who gets himself killed for his country. He believes it is important to distinguish between suicide and sacrifice. Perhaps this is so, but it is a difficult area. Most people, whether they are Christians or not, would not consider as suicide the fatal decision of Jesus of Nazareth to enter Jerusalem in the full knowledge that he would be crucified. On the other hand many of us would be prepared to call the action of Captain Oates, when he walked out of his tent to die in the snow, a case of suicide, even although it was intended as a sacrifice to save the lives of his colleagues on Scott's expedition to the Antarctic. The important point to emerge from Halbwachs' deliberations on definitions is that the chief factor will always be the attitude adopted by society.

Before leaving the subject of definitions brief reference must be made to *parasuicide*. This term was introduced by Kreitman[8] in 1969 and is defined as a non-fatal act in which an individual deliberately causes self-injury or ingests a substance in excess of any prescribed or generally recognized therapeutic dosage. The need for a special term arises because a great many instances of self-harm appear not to have the intention of being fatal. If this is the case it would be inappropriate to speak of *attempted suicide*. Even the term *deliberate self-poisoning*, which had been suggested by Kessel[9] a few years earlier, could be misleading in certain cases, for example where a quantity of non-toxic substance has been swallowed in the mistaken belief that it would be harmful. It is desirable to distinguish between failed suicide attempts and cases which have the same outcome but which were not intended to be fatal. To be specific, we may on the one hand have an elderly person who leaves a suicide note and then takes double the prescribed dose of sleeping tablets with the clear intention of dying; on the other hand we could have someone who takes a large number of tranquillizers but arranges that someone will be sure to intervene. Both wake up in hospital the next day: one was an attempted suicide; the other can best be described as a parasuicide. The relationship between these two kinds of act is not at all clear and will be dealt with in Chapter 7.

Having thus cleared the way, we can now proceed to look at what the figures tell us. The information referred to is given in the Appendix. You may wish to refer to it intermittently as you read what follows or you may prefer to peruse the tables and graphs later. What follows can be readily understood without a study of the data. The figures for suicide rate are given in terms of number of deaths per 100,000 of the population. This means that these figures can, with the reservations already stated, be compared regardless of the sizes of the populations concerned.

The first observation to be made is that over reasonably long periods the suicide rate for a given country is remarkably stable. One has to ask why this should be so. After all, suicide is a private act and so one would expect the key factor to be something to do with the psychology of the individual. What the figures seem to be telling us is that the proportion of the population who will commit suicide is predictable. This would be like the figures the insurance companies are able to use as a basis for their very lucrative business. The fact is that some of us live to a healthy old age, some die in infancy and between is a whole spectrum of ages of mortality. Actuaries cannot predict the demise of any individual, but they are able to arrive at reliable estimates of the average mortality for a given age band of the whole population.

The second point to be made, however, is that the rates given for suicide vary significantly from one country to another. Now, as has already been mentioned, this might partly stem from differences in the procedures for recording cause of death, but it hardly seems likely that differences of the kind observed (Tables

1 and 2) could be explained in this way. For example, there must be some other explanation for the very high rate in Hungary, forty per 100,000 against three per 100,000 for Greece (Table 2). Another distinctive feature revealed (Table 2) is the wide spread in the ratios of males to females. In many countries this ratio is not far from two to one, but in Poland it is over five to one, with Finland and Iceland close behind with ratios just over four to one; in Northern Ireland, however, the number of women who take their own lives is almost equal to the number of men who do so.

Another interesting feature of the statistics is that there are certain very clear moves in the number of suicides, which appear to coincide with political events or social upheaval. An examination of the figures for England and Wales for the period from 1901 to 1984 (Diagram 1) shows that there was a marked decline during the two world wars and a peak during the years of the Depression in the early thirties. It has been suggested that the drops in the numbers of suicides recorded during the wars might at least partly have been the consequence of temporary changes in the system for reporting cause of death. It has also been recognized that many suicides were not brought to light in wartime because they were concealed among deaths incurred in battle. Neither of these explanations is satisfactory. Durkheim showed that drops in the suicide rate had occurred in several other wars and he pointed out that victor and vanquished were equally affected. Moreover the return to the pre-war rate appears to be relatively gradual rather than a sudden increase when hostilities cease. Halbwachs noted that the decline in suicide rate during war was not confined to the belligerent countries.

All these facts seem to support the view that the incidence of suicide is influenced by factors external to the individual. Thus Durkheim was able to describe the social causes of self-destruction. Here we move into the realm of theory, but the evidence for a relationship between suicide rate and certain social conditions seems to be strong. (Whether it is correct to speak of social *causes* is a question we shall examine in the next chapter.) It is perhaps unnecessary to produce further statistical evidence but there is one more interesting relationship to be noted which most convincingly demonstrates that the suicide rate is subject to external influence. Durkheim observed that the majority of suicides occur during the daytime, more taking place in the late morning and in the afternoon than at any other time of the day or night. He noted, too, that in all European countries 'beginning with January inclusive the incidence of suicide increases regularly from month to month until about June and regularly decreases from that time to the end of the year.'[6] This conclusion is borne out most convincingly by figures for England and Wales. Here data for five ten-year periods have been plotted on a monthly basis (Diagram 2) to reveal that there is a consistent tendency for suicides to be most frequent at that time of year when we might have expected the frequency to be at its lowest, in the spring. People take their own lives at all times of the year and at all times of the day and night. This is as one might expect. If there were to be a peak time one might reasonably have felt that it would occur at some period when our own experience tells us our spirits are at a low ebb, say in the early hours of the morning at one of the bleaker times of the year, the onset of winter or in the depth of that period when the nights are long and the days sunless. But this is not so. The peak consistently comes between April and June.

Reference has already been made to the disparity in the suicide rates for men and women. Not only are these rates different but the extent to which they differ varies with time. Thus in 1901 there were in England and Wales three male suicides for every one woman who took her own life. By 1945 the ratio had changed to two to one. By 1974 the gap had narrowed still further, with fewer than three men taking their own lives for every two female suicides. Since then the disparity has tended to increase again and in 1983 the ratio was almost back to the 1945 level of two to one.

The figures that are available allow us to draw some interesting conclusions about the influence of marital status. When the numbers of men and women who took their own lives in the period 1970-72 are examined it becomes clear that those who are married are significantly less likely to commit suicide than are the single. The risk for the divorced and widowed, however, is higher than for either the married or the unmarried. These observations apply to men and women of all ages, though the advantage held by married men and women in the 15 to 24 age group is relatively small. When one examines the effect of age on the suicide rate it is necessary to take account of the age distribution of the population. Thus there are two ways of looking at the figures. One is to split the population into age bands and compare the numbers of suicides for each. (Table 3 shows the figures presented in this way for 1983.) It is then possible to establish, for example, that although the percentage of suicides who kill themselves in their middle years, that is from 35 to 69, is almost the same for men and women (about 60 per cent), the figure for the younger group of men (34 and under) is almost double that for the women (27 per cent against 14 per cent). For the older group (70 and over) the position is reversed (24 per cent for women and 13 for men). The other way of looking at the age figures is to present them as the number of suicides per 100,000 in each age bracket. Whereas the first method tells us *how many* men and/or women in the population die in each age group, the second method tells us the *rate* for each age group. As would be expected the rate for those in their teens is relatively low. As we move up the age scale, however, the rate for both men and women rises. After the age of 70 or so it begins to decline for women. For men it appears to turn down a year or so later, though if accidental and open-verdict deaths are included there is no such decline; the inclusion of accidental and open-verdict deaths does not substantially alter the picture for women.

Attempts to detect a variation in suicide rate across the range of employment status are not wholly convincing. A study[10] of the figures for the period of 1961-74 considered the five groups: (I) professional, (II) lower professional and executive, (III) skilled, including both manual and non-manual, (IV) semi-skilled and (V) unskilled. There was evidence of a higher than expected suicide rate for group (V) and also to a lesser extent for groups (I) and (IV). There was evidence of differences in age distribution of the deaths, the higher rate in group (I) being found in those over 35; the higher rates for groups (IV) and (V) were found especially to be in the younger age groups. The report[11] of the study of data between 1950 and 1982, however, concluded that the results of studies carried out around the census years 1951, 1961 and 1971 'show very little consistent variation by social class'. The same report considered the possible effects of unemployment and concluded that 'over the complete period there is no symmetry in the peaks and troughs of the numbers of suicides at all ages of males and the curve of unemployment.' It mentioned however, that another study had shown a higher than expected rate of suicide among the sick and those inactive for other reasons; the report went on to note that 'there is an association between chronic illness and the likelihood of an individual being made redundant.' Thus even if there were a clear connection between unemployment and suicide it would be difficult to establish whether unemployment is the cause. Discussion with those who are suicidal gives the impression, however, that, if not the prime cause of their dispiritment, it is often a contributing factor.

Comparison of the figures for urban and rural areas suggests that, broadly speaking, the higher the population the higher is the suicide rate likely to be (Table 4). The figures on which this conclusion is based are taken from two periods, 1959 to 1963 and 1970 to 1972, and both sets support this conclusion with two exceptions. The first is that the rate for men in rural areas is higher than that for small urban communities in 1970 to 1972. A possible reason for this is that rural areas showed a smaller drop in the suicide rate in the sixties than occurred elsewhere. The second is that there is a higher rate for women in the medium-sized urban areas than would be expected if the pattern were consistent. There is no obvious explanation for this, but it does not seem to invalidate the overall picture.

Finally, the statistics of suicide can tell us something about the methods used to commit it. Probably the most significant factors in determining the ways people choose to kill themselves are the desire to minimize the pain involved and the availability of the means. Twenty-five years ago almost half the suicides in this country, both male and female, used domestic gas. In those days 'putting your head in the gas oven' was common parlance for suicide. It was certainly one of the most convenient methods. The gas supplied to most homes was derived from coal and it contained over 10 per cent carbon monoxide, which is capable of causing unconsciousness and death. In the sixties there was a change in the provenance of domestic gas, the old coal gas being replaced mainly by gas from the North Sea oil fields and this was substantially free from carbon monoxide. Throughout the decade there was a reduction in the average carbon monoxide level in town gas and with it came a steady fall in the use of gas for suicide. By the mid-seventies the practice had virtually ceased. Carbon monoxide is also a constituent of motor car exhaust gas and, not surprisingly, throughout the period when coal gas was being replaced there was an increase in suicides achieved by breathing exhaust fumes. The rate of increase in suicides by this method was faster than could have been explained merely by the growth in the number of private cars. Its use, however, has largely been confined to men.

A look at the figures for the methods used by male and female suicides in 1980 (Table 5) shows that for men the most common was hanging. This has always been so. Perhaps it is chosen because it is unlikely to fail and the means are usually at hand. Close behind hanging comes poisoning by solid or liquid substances. The materials most often used are drugs provided for medical purposes. These include freely available products such as aspirin and paracetamol, both of which can be lethal in overdose. Drugs obtainable only on prescription are also employed; they include analgesics, tranquillizers and antidepressants. Barbiturates have frequently been used but are now less often available than they once were. After poisoning men seem to favour the use of exhaust gas referred to above. The use of firearms comes next. Availability is clearly a factor limiting the adoption of this method. In the USA, where access to guns is more widespread than here, suicide by shooting is much more common. In California almost half the suicides are achieved by means of firearms; in certain other states, such as Wyoming and Montana the proportion is over 90 per cent. [12] After shooting, the next most common method for men in this country is drowning. Perhaps surprisingly in view of the frequent references to it in allusions to suicide, jumping from high places comes very low on the list, accounting for less than 5 per cent of male suicides.

The picture for women is somewhat different. Overdoses of drugs come at the top of the list and account for just over half of all female suicides. Next is the method referred to as hanging, strangulation and suffocation, but here, whereas hanging accounts for 90 per cent of male deaths in this category, it appears that many women resort to the use of plastic bags as a means of suffocation. Another difference between the methods chosen by women and those adopted by men is that the proportion of female suicides which are accomplished by drowning is more than double that for men.

One is always tempted to theorize about possible reasons for the choice of methods and the differences between those used by men and those opted for by women. It would not, however, be profitable to do so. Perhaps it is better to let the facts speak for themselves and move on to consider some of the possible causes of suicidal behaviour.

2.

THE SOCIAL CONTEXT

Each society is predisposed to contribute a definite quota of voluntary deaths.

Emile Durkheim, *Le Suicide*

Durkheim subtitled his book, 'A Study in Sociology.' It was one of the first examples of the methodical examination of statistical data as a means of exploring the social factors at play in human behaviour. It remains a classic of its kind and even though it was written over eighty years ago the conclusions it reached are still of interest to us today. This is not to say that they are universally accepted. Halbwachs, to whom reference has already been made, shared many but not all of Durkheim's views. In particular he did not agree with the notion that there is a fundamental difference between the social *causes* and the psychological *motives* of suicide. Durkheim believed that cause was to be found in the underlying social conditions and that the subjective reasons for a suicidal act were no more than the trigger. True, the victim might feel that the loss of a loved one left only one course of action, but the actual cause was to be found elsewhere. Not surprisingly there was strong opposition to this view and it came especially from those who believed that the cause of suicide was to be found in the individual's psychological make-up. It was held by some that suicide is almost invariably found among people of a certain temperament. Halbwachs' contribution was to question both theses. In his opinion it was necessary to abandon the idea that suicide is caused either by mental disorder on the one hand or by social factors on the other. 'It is unnecessary', he wrote, 'to believe that there are two categories of suicide, each explained by a different determinism, or that, depending on the individual, the organic determinism is sometimes in play, and sometimes the social determinism. Actually the suicide, every suicide, can be envisioned from two points of view. Depending on whether one places himself at one or the other, he will see in the suicide the effect of a nervous trouble arising from organic causes, or of a rupture of the collective equilibrium resulting from social causes.'[7]

Durkheim's approach was to eliminate in turn each of the possible causes of suicide by citing statistical evidence to show that they could not account for the facts. In the end he was left with his thesis that suicide was a social phenomenon. He began by attacking the then widely held views that suicide was a disease in its own right or that it was an event involved in certain types of insanity. Against the first of these he argued that there was no evidence to support the existence of suicidal or any other type of monomania. Considering the second possibility, he enumerated four categories of suicide of the insane. The first, which he called *maniacal suicide*, was due to hallucination, the victim killing himself to escape an imaginary danger or in obedience to mysterious instructions he believed he had been given. The second category, described as *melancholy suicide*, was associated with a general state of deep depression in which the sufferer had lost a normal perception of the bonds that connected him with the people and things around him. Thirdly Durkheim referred to *obsessive suicide*, which arose from a fixed idea of self-destruction that took hold of the victim's mind. Finally there was *impulsive or automatic suicide*, which resulted from a sudden irresistible impulse. All suicides of the insane, argued Durkheim, were characterized by the absence of any real motive and so the undoubted occurrence of suicides where such motives were clearly present proved that not all suicides could be attributed to insanity. He then demonstrated that there was good statistical reason for believing that there is no consistent connection between suicide and mental alienation. By a similar procedure he eliminated the possibility of causes based on alcoholism or alcohol-induced mental disease.

Durkheim went on to examine the effects of race, heredity, geographic location and climate, but found that none of these provided the cause. He also examined the suggestion that suicide might be the subject of imitation. 'The idea of suicide may undoubtedly be communicated by contagion', wrote Durkheim. There have certainly been many notable examples. Take for instance the case of Miss Kiyoko Matsumoto, a 19-year-old Japanese girl who in February 1933 jumped into the volcano of Mihara-Yama on Oshima. Until that date no notoriety was attached to this location, but in the remaining ten months of the year no fewer than 143 people killed themselves there. On one day alone there were six successful suicides and twenty-five attempts. In the following year 167 suicides took place at Mihara-Yama. Fedden, whose book, *Suicide*,[13] was the source of this example, mentioned also that various books have been said to have resulted in suicide, including Goethe's *Werther*, Byron's *Manfred*, Chateaubriand's *René*, Lamartine's *Raphael* and Vigny's *Chatterton*. In his view, however, contagion was an incidental rather than a prime factor and resulted in the death only of those destined for suicide anyway. Such, broadly speaking, were the conclusions of Durkheim. 'With very rare exceptions, then,' he wrote, 'it may be said that imitation is not an original factor of suicide. It only exposes a state which is the true generating cause of the act and which probably would have produced its natural effect even had imitation not intervened; for the predisposition must be very strong to enable so slight a matter to translate it into action.'[6] This is what his examination of the available statistics revealed and so he was able to conclude, 'It is not surprising, therefore, that the acts fail to show the stamp of imitation, since it has no influence of its own, and what it does exert is very slight.'[6] (This is an important point and it is relevant to the modern view that to speak about suicide to a potential victim is not going to stimulate thoughts of self-destruction he does not already have. This question will be dealt with in Chapter 10.)

Moving on to consider the social factors that might influence the incidence of suicide, Durkheim identified three categories. The first of these, which he labelled *egoistic suicide*, emerged from his study of religious affiliation, marriage and the family, and political and national communities. A comparison of the suicide rates for the adherents of different religious sects led him to a number of conclusions about the influence of religion. There undoubtedly was a preventative effect but this was not due, as many had believed, to the fact that religion condemned suicide more clearly than did secular morality, but *because it was a society*. 'What constitutes this society is the existence of a certain number of beliefs and practices common to all the faithful,' wrote Durkheim. 'The details of dogmas and rites are secondary. The essential thing is that they be capable of supporting a sufficiently intense collective life.' It also appeared from these studies that as a rule suicide increased with knowledge. This, Durkheim contended, was due to 'the weakening of traditional beliefs and to the state of moral individualism resulting' from it. The reason why Protestantism was less prophylactic of suicide than either Judaism or Roman Catholicism was the process of secularization and the resulting disintegration of the ties of the individual to the group. 'Suicide', he concluded, 'varies inversely with the degree of integration of religious society.'[6]

Durkheim's investigation of the relationship between suicide and the family led to a similar conclusion: an inverse relationship between suicide and the degree of integration of domestic society. At first sight it appeared that suicide was less frequent among the unmarried, but further examination revealed the opposite to be the case. The reason for the discrepancy was that a very significant proportion of the unmarried are under the age of 16 and so fall into that group in which suicide is very rare for reasons quite unconnected with their single status. When Durkheim excluded the under-16s he saw that the married had less tendency towards suicide than had the single, or, as he put it, they enjoyed a 'coefficient of preservation' in comparison with unmarried persons. He noted, however, that too early marriage had an aggravating influence on the suicide rate, especially among men. From the age of 20 onwards the benefit of marriage became apparent for both sexes, though the extent to which the married were less prone to suicide than the single was not the same for both sexes. This variation between the sexes differed from one society to another. The death of a marriage partner increased the likelihood of suicide but the rate for widows and widowers was found to be generally lower than for the unmarried. Once again the difference between the sexes in this respect varied from one society to another. Turning his attention to the question of children Durkheim was able to conclude that their contribution to the coefficient of preservation enjoyed by the married was of great importance. He suggested that a possible reason for the apparently adverse effect of too early marriage was the fact that the young, having been married for only a short period, had in general insufficient time to have had children. He noted also that in France married but childless women were more liable to commit suicide than were unmarried women of the same age. It was his view that the relative immunity of the married to suicide arose less from conjugal society than from family society. Moreover he found that the greater the 'density' of the family the lower was the tendency towards suicide. Or to put it another way: the more powerfully integrated the family is, the greater is the protection it affords against suicide.

Applied to political society the concept of integration appeared equally relevant. Durkheim felt that there was only one explanation for the decline in the suicide rate during periods of war and great social disturbance. These occurrences aroused collective sentiments such as patriotism and partisan spirit, political and national faith. Thus they concentrated activity towards a single end and so for a time at least brought about a stronger integration of society. This led Durkheim to this third proposition, namely that suicide varies inversely with the degree of integration of political society.

Consideration of the possible reasons for the aggravation of the suicide rate by a reduction in the integration of religious, domestic and political society led Durkheim to the recognition of the first of his three categories of suicide already referred to, namely *egoistic suicide*:

> Society cannot disintegrate without the individual simultaneously detaching himself from social life, without his own goals becoming preponderant over those of the community, in a word without his personality tending to surmount the collective personality. The more weakened the groups to which he belongs, the less he depends on them, the more he consequently depends on himself and recognizes no other rules of conduct than what are founded on his private interests. If we agree to call this state egoism, in which the individual ego asserts itself to excess, we may call egoistic the special type of suicide springing from excessive individualism.[6]

The bond that attaches the individual to society, thought Durkheim, also unites him with life. Each of us receives moral support from our relationship with a strongly cohesive society and we are able to share the collective energy instead of being thrown back on our individual resources. In other words we are social beings with social needs, and to become isolated from society is a deprivation for that part of our being that needs attachment to something external to itself. '. . . the bond attaching man to life relaxes because that attaching him to society is itself slack,' writes Durkheim. He continues:

> The incidents of private life which seem the direct inspiration of suicide and are considered its determining causes are in reality only incidental causes. The individual yields to the slightest shock of circumstances because the state of society has made him a ready prey to suicide.'[6]

The second category of suicide identified by Durkheim was *altruistic suicide*. He went on to differentiate three sub-categories, which he designated *obligatory, optional* and *acute* altruistic suicide. The first of these was characterized by the expectation of society that the person in question should take his own life; it was his duty to do so. This obligatory altruistic suicide was, observed Durkheim, common among primitive peoples and there were three main types. The first was the suicide of men on the threshold of old age or stricken with sickness. As an example Durkheim quoted that Danish warriors had considered it a disgrace to die in bed of old age or sickness and that they therefore killed themselves to avoid this ignominy. The second type was the suicide of women on the deaths of their husbands as exemplified by the practice of suttee, which was at one time common in India and to which reference has already been made in Chapter 1. The third type was the suicide of followers or servants on the death of their chiefs. Here Durkheim referred[6] to Henri Martin, author of *Histoire de France*, who declared that the funerals of chiefs in Gaul 'were bloody hecatombs where their garments, weapons, horses and favourite slaves were solemnly burned, together with the personal followers who had not died in the chief's last battle'. If any of those groups of people had refused to die they would have lost the respect of those around them. In other words, society spoke the sentence of death and this was imposed for social ends or because of religious beliefs. Durkheim saw this category of suicide as being quite different from that which he had labelled *egoistic*. Whereas the latter was due to excessive individuation in which society allowed the individual to escape, becoming insufficiently integrated, obligatory altruistic suicide was the result of the close control society had over the individual. The goal of the victim of egoistic suicide was to do with the individual; that of altruistic suicide was exterior to the individual and was in some way related to the social group.

Because not all altruistic suicides were obligatory Durkheim found it necessary to use the term *optional* to describe certain types where the victim was not explicitly forced to take his own life. Public opinion did not demand suicide but was favourably disposed to it. Whereas the person who did *not* comply with the demands of the society which regarded his death as obligatory met with disapproval, the victim of optional altruistic suicide was considered praiseworthy. Thus in many primitive societies people took their own lives for the slightest of reasons, for example to escape the stigma of insult.

The third type of altruistic suicide, designated *acute*, arose because the victim killed himself for the joy of sacrifice. Unlike the obligatory type, where death was expected, and the optional where some situation had occurred to detract from the value the victim attached to his life, the acute altruistic suicide was the consequence of the view that the renunciation of life was in itself praiseworthy. Durkheim cited as examples the Hindu custom of seeking death in the waters of the Ganges and the Jain practice of religious suicide in which the victim allowed himself to die of hunger. Of this type of suicide Durkheim said:

> We actually see the individual in all these cases seek to strip himself of his personal being in order to be engulfed in something which he regards as his true essence. The name he gives it is unimportant; he feels that he exists in it and in it alone, and strives so violently to blend himself with it in order to have being. He must therefore consider that he has no life of his own. Impersonality is here carried to its highest pitch; altruism is acute. [6]

Durkheim was of the opinion that altruistic suicide was primarily a feature of the lower societies, but he recognized that it could also be found in more recent societies and he went on to refer to the slaughter of Christian martyrs. He believed that all those who voluntarily allowed themselves to be killed were in fact suicides. Halbwachs did not agree and indeed he regarded most of the acts that Durkheim called altruistic suicide to be more properly described as self-sacrifice. He made special reference to Durkheim's discussion of suicide among soldiers, which in all European countries had been found to be more prevalent than suicide in the civilian population. From a study of the statistics Durkheim concluded that disgust with the service was not the cause. 'The members of the army most stricken by suicide', he wrote, 'are also those who are most inclined to this career, who are best suited to its needs and are best sheltered from its disadvantages and inconveniences. The coefficient of aggravation special to this profession is then caused not by the repugnance it inspires, but, on the contrary, by the sum total of states, acquired habits or natural dispositions making up the military spirit.' [6] Durkheim went on to argue that the soldier was trained to set little value upon himself and that he must be prepared to sacrifice himself if ordered to do so. Thus, the soldier had to have a relatively weak tie binding himself to his individuality. 'In short, a soldier's principle of action is external to himself; which is the quality of the state of altruism. Of all elements constituting our modern society, the army, indeed, most recalls the structure of lower societies.'

Although not all army suicides were necessarily altruistic, Durkheim felt that all the evidence pointed to military suicide as being a form of altruistic suicide. Halbwachs quoted[7] the comment made by the French philosopher Henri Bergson soon after the appearance of Durkheim's book: 'It may not be necessary to search so far. Actually, it is very well understood why soldiers, especially old soldiers, kill themselves more often than do other men: they are bored.' One is reminded of Charles Caleb Colton's observation that 'ennui has made more gamblers than avarice, more drunkards than thirst, and perhaps as many suicides as despair.'[14] Another simple explanation for the higher rate of suicide among soldiers was that they did not fail at it. The two methods of suicide they adopted most frequently were hanging and the use of firearms and these were, Halbwachs pointed out, the most often successful.

Durkheim's third category of suicide was given the name *anomic*. The word *anomie* is used to describe a condition of hopelessness caused by breakdown of rules of conduct and loss of belief and sense of purpose; it can be applied to the individual and to the society. Durkheim observed that economic crises had an aggravating effect on the suicidal tendency. This applied to fortunate crises as well as to disastrous ones and the reason, Durkheim said, was the disturbing effect such crises had on the collective order. Egoistic suicide resulted from a man's no longer having a basis for existence in life. Altruistic suicide was caused by the individual finding the basis of existence to be situated beyond life itself. Anomic suicide, Durkheim said, resulted from man's activity lacking regulation and from the suffering that ensued. Economic crises might well have been thought to increase the tendency to suicide because the resulting poverty leads to hardship, but this explanation was not supported by the facts. As Durkheim pointed out, if voluntary deaths increased because life was becoming more difficult one would expect them to diminish as comfort increased. This did not occur. The cause of suicide in times of economic crisis was the change in the individual's horizon. This could contract as a result of greatly reduced economic circumstances or, through a sudden increase in wealth, it could be broadened so much that the individual was no longer able to cope with the new opportunities that were offered to him.

At every moment of history there is a dim perception, in the moral consciousness of societies, of the respective value of different social services, the relative reward due to each, and the consequent degree of comfort appropriate on the average to workers in each occupation.

Thus, according to Durkheim, everyone vaguely realized the limits set to his ambitions. Man, he suggested, was governed by a conscience greater than his own; he was subject to society:

Poverty protects against suicide because it is a restraint in itself. No matter how one acts, desires have to depend upon resources to some extent; actual possessions are partly the criterion of those aspired to. So the less one has the less he is tempted to extend the range of his needs indefinitely. Lack of power, compelling moderation, accustoms men to it, while nothing excites envy if no one has superfluity. Wealth, on the other hand, by the power it bestows, deceives us into believing that we depend on ourselves only. Reducing the resistance we encounter from objects, it suggests the possibility of unlimited success against them. The less limited one feels, the more intolerable all limitation appears. Not without reason, therefore, have so many religions dwelt on the advantage and moral value of poverty.

Thus, Durkheim maintained, anomic suicide resulted partly from crises causing upheavals in the economic climate. But there was also a more or less steady contribution to the suicide rate depending on the extent to which society engendered feelings of dissatisfaction.

He recognized that it was not only the economic situation that was responsible for anomic suicide. There was a domestic anomie that arose from widowhood and through the break-up of a marriage by divorce. He noted that the incidence of suicide amongst divorced persons of both sexes was between three and four times that for married people. This was because divorce ended the regulative influence of marital society on both partners. The effect on the male partner was, however, much more marked and this was, Durkheim held, because it was the man who benefited most from the regulation provided by matrimony. As he pointed out, the cause of the difference between the sexes in the effect of divorce on the suicide rate was the fact that the needs of the spouses were not the same: 'their interests are contrary; one needs restraint and the other liberty.'[6]

In a footnote to his discussion of anomic suicide Durkheim made a brief reference to a fourth type of suicide, which he called *fatalistic* suicide. 'It is the suicide deriving from excessive regulation, that of persons with futures pitilessly blocked and passions violently choked by oppressive discipline. It is the suicide of very young husbands, of the married woman who is childless.' He felt, however, that this fourth type was of little contemporary importance and examples were hard to find apart from the two cases referred to in the passage quoted. He suggested that the suicides of slaves might come under this heading, being attributable to excessive physical or moral despotism. The name he gave to it was intended 'to bring out the ineluctable and inflexible nature of a rule against which there is no appeal'.[6]

There is much in Durkheim's thesis that we might be tempted to accept, and certainly he illuminated much of value, drawing our attention to several factors and influences. Having read his arguments, however, are we yet able to say with any degree of certainty why the suicide rate in present-day Hungary is so much higher than in most other countries, or why the ratio of male to female suicides should not be one to one, or why it should be so very much higher in Poland than it is in Ireland? We can venture theories to account for these differences but each one will inevitably run into difficulty somewhere. This is because the reasons are always extremely complex. However, the very fact that there *are* differences between societies is some justification for Durkheim's approach.

So far as the difference between the sexes is concerned we are not much further forward. Durkheim suggested, for example, that one reason why women were less likely than men to take their own lives when bereavement robbed them of their marriage partners was because they could endure life in isolation more easily than could men.

It is said that woman's affective faculties, being very intense, are easily employed outside the domestic circle, while her devotion is indispensable to man to help him to endure life. Actually, if this is her privilege it is because her sensibility is rudimentary rather than highly developed. As she lives outside of community existence more than man, she is less penetrated by it; society is less necessary to her because she is less impregnated with sociability. She has few needs in this direction and satisfies them easily.[6]

One wonders how many would agree with Durkheim's sentiments today, especially when he continues:

With a few devotional practices and some animals to care for, the old unmarried woman's life is full. If she remains faithfully attached to religious traditions and thus finds ready protection against suicide it is because these very simple social forms satisfy all her needs. Man, on the contrary, is hard beset in this respect. As his thought and activity develop, they increasingly overflow these antiquated forms. But then he needs others. Because he is a more complex social being, he can maintain his equilibrium only by finding more points of support outside himself, and it is because his moral balance depends on a larger number of conditions that it is more easily disturbed.

One cannot but feel that, however much truth they may hold for certain societies, these arguments would be regarded by many as untenable. Indeed Durkheim's basic thesis that the *cause* of suicide was social has to be questioned. This is not to dispute, however, that social conditions exert an influence on the suicide rate. As was indicated at the beginning of this chapter, Halbwachs saw things somewhat differently from Durkheim. He did not dispute the social dimension; nor did he hold the extreme opposite view that suicide was almost always associated with some kind of mental disturbance. He thought, as had Durkheim, that it was reasonable to use the statistics of suicide as an approach to understanding what lay behind this action but he did not agree with the notion that one need go no further than sociology for explanation.

'Why,' asked Fedden in his book *Suicide — A Social and Historical Study*,[13] 'when faced with certain difficulties in a certain social framework, will a man make the extraordinary gesture of taking his own life, rather than evolve some other defence?' Certainly the act runs contrary to the instinct for self-preservation. Fedden wondered if the consistency of the figures for suicide did not indicate that there was a natural desire for death working itself out. Freud had, outlined a theory of the death instinct. He had inferred from his studies of human behaviour that the most fundamental of all instincts was a compulsion to repetition, which he described as 'a tendency innate in living organic matter impelling it towards the reinstatement of an earlier condition'.[15] This goal was the 'ancient starting point', the equilibrium of death. 'If we may assume as an experience admitting of no exception that everything living dies from causes within itself and returns to the inorganic, we can only say "The goal of all life is death", and, casting back, "The inanimate was there before the animate"'.[15]

Psychiatrists speak of *libido*, that is the energy of the life instinct, the purpose of which seems to be the preservation of the race, and *mortido*, the energy of the death instinct. The greatest satisfaction of mortido is achieved in murder and suicide and its purpose seems to be the preservation of the individual. 'In most people's lives', wrote Eric Berne in his *Layman's Guide to Psychiatry and Psychoanalysis*,[16] 'such extremes are not found. Libido and mortido are well controlled and hidden by each other and possibly by other forces, so that many people go through life without realizing how powerful these two urges are and how much they influence motives and conduct.'

Here, then, we have two explanations of suicide, the influence of social conditions and the imbalance of the tensions between libido and mortido. Each acts at least partly beyond the awareness of the individual. And yet the individual may have, indeed usually has, his own perceptions of what has driven him to the point of ultimate despair. The reasons or motives for self-destruction are legion. Each suicidal person is the victim of something that troubles him. 'A trait is common to them all, however,' wrote Halbwachs:

> None perceives more of society than its hostile aspects, its steepest slopes. The term *motives* must be retained for these events: mental illness, loss of money, mourning, or love-pangs, since they are so many different particular forms hiding the same condition. The unique cause of suicide, however, is the condition itself, that is, a feeling of a solitude which is definitive and without remedy. It is too easy to say, this man killed himself because he was manic-depressive, the other because of heavy money losses, etc. That is a somewhat crude kind of narration which sticks only to the most apparent and the most uncommon facts. Such explanations would be meaningless unless what determined the suicide in the nervous disorder was precisely what characterizes the loss of money. That is, one must extract from the former the condition of anguish and depression in which the person exposed to destitution and downfall is likewise found. It is, however, abundantly evident that the nervous disorder would not lead to suicide if it were not at all accompanied by this condition. It is because the same condition appears in both cases that the suicide occurs.[7]

That phrase of Halbwachs, 'a feeling of solitude which is definitive and without remedy', seems to pinpoint the underlying motive common to a great many suicides. It is a sense of isolation that can arise from an event or circumstances or disturbance in the life of an individual. This same sense of isolation can be engendered by social conditions or, to look at it another way, some social environments are less likely than others to protect the individual from such feelings of solitude. 'Suicide', said Fedden, 'is the act of the solitary.'[13] Solitude can be the result of something within the individual or it can be caused by some external factor in the social milieu, or, as is probable in a great many cases, by both.

This is a convenient point at which to leave the social dimension of the subject. The sociologist looks at suicide from the outside and in a sense the psychiatrist has to do likewise. Both approaches are scientific. They treat their material objectively and there is an inevitable clinical distancing from what suicide is all about, like using forceps to pick up something unpleasant. This is in no way intended to be derogatory of these methodologies. Both have an essential part to play in our understanding of suicide. But there is another equally valid viewpoint: that of the artist. He can help us to enter the thoughts of the suicidal person as perhaps no other can. Ideally one should seek the views of the victim, but we are at his mercy, for often he tells us only what he wishes us to know. As Durkheim said,

> How discover the agent's motive and whether he desired death itself when he formed his resolve, or had some other purpose? Intent is too intimate a thing to be more than approximately interpreted by another. It even escapes self-observation. How often we mistake the true reason for our acts! We constantly explain acts due to petty feelings or blind routine by generous passions or lofty considerations.[6]

As we shall see in Chapter 3 the subjective reasons are often clearly perceived but perhaps just as often they are confused.

3.

THE ROOTS OF DESPAIR

It will be lonely to be dead, but it cannot be much more lonely than to be alive.

Axel Munthe, *The Story of San Michele*

Here we move from notions of causes and influences to look at motives and intentions, from facts and theories to thoughts and feelings. However real and powerful may be the pressures exerted on the individual by his social environment, however painful and hopeless his personal circumstances, suicide is never the necessary outcome. Between the external provocations and the final, desperate act of self-destruction there is an inner conflict between the will to live and the urge to die. 'Our greatest foes, and whom we must chiefly combat', wrote Cervantes in his great novel, *Don Quixote*, 'are within.'[17] Albert Camus tells of an apartment manager who had killed himself:

> I was told that he had lost his daughter five years before, that he had changed greatly since and that that experience had 'undermined' him. A more exact word cannot be imagined. Beginning to think is beginning to be undermined. Society has but little connection with such beginnings. The worm is in man's heart.[2]

The thought of self-annihilation is common enough. One can philosophize on the merits of oblivion or contemplate in a wholly theoretical fashion the circumstances that might lead us to reject life. Morbid notions may be entertained when the present is disagreeable or the future seems to hold no promise. In moments of depression we may, like Shakespeare's Hamlet, wish:

O! that this too too solid flesh would melt,
Thaw and resolve itself into a dew;
Or that the Everlasting had not fix'd
His canon 'gainst self-slaughter! O God! O God!
How weary, stale, flat, and unprofitable
Seem to me all the uses of this world.*

Fortunately, for most of us such moods are short-lived, and with their passing, equanimity returns. Some people, however, find that these dark thoughts recur and they are troubled by them. The possibility that they might 'do something foolish' is frightening. It is almost as if they cannot trust themselves to survive, like the person who avoids standing close to the edge of a cliff or railway platform for fear that he might involuntarily throw himself over. There is no suicidal urge, only the anxiety that there might be. For others the suicidal urge is all too real, though its duration may be measured in minutes or hours rather than in the days or weeks that their black moods occupy. For them it seems that, in Durkheim's words, 'if life is not worth the trouble of being lived, everything becomes a pretext to rid [themselves] of it.'⁶ Somehow the idea of suicide establishes itself in their minds just as a cancer might grow in their bodies. From time to time their thoughts of suicide spill over into self-destructive urges and, perhaps, to fatal action. It is rare for determined self-destructive action to be an impulse that has not been preceded by thoughts and urges over a period of days or longer.

In his novel, *Anna Karenina*,¹⁸ Tolstoy depicts three characters with suicidal thoughts, all quite different: Levin, Count Vronsky and Anna herself. Levin is a sincere, uncomplicated sort of person, much more at home in the country among the peasants than in the sophisticated social milieu of Moscow. His offer of marriage having been rejected by the young Kitty, he returns to his country estate and throws himself into its management, convinced that he will never wed. Much later he is able to marry Kitty and they have a child, so it would appear that he now has no cause for sorrow and that he can be happy and fulfilled. But this is not so. We learn that 'Levin, a happy father and husband, in perfect health, was several times so near to suicide that he had to hide a rope lest he be tempted to hang himself, and would not go out with a gun for fear of shooting himself.' He is tormented by his

---

* This and all other Shakespeare quotations are from the Oxford edition, 1945.

want of faith. The beliefs of his childhood have deserted him. One night long before his marriage he had lain in bed listening to his brother, a sick man, coughing and struggling for breath, muttering 'Oh God!' and 'Ah, the devil!'

Death, the inevitable end of everything, confronted him for the first time with irresistible force. And death, which was here in this beloved brother who groaned in his sleep and from force of habit invoked without distinction both God and the devil, was not so remote as it had hitherto seemed to him. He felt it in himself too. If not today, then tomorrow; if not tomorrow, then in thirty years' time — wasn't it all the same? And what this inevitable death was, he not only did not know, not only had never considered, but could not and dared not consider. 'Here am I working, wanting to accomplish something, and completely forgetting it must all end — that there is such a thing as death.'

Later when he and Kitty stand by his brother's bedside, having watched him die, Levin feels again 'that sense of horror in face of the enigma' and he is 'even more incapable of apprehending the meaning of death; its inevitability rises up before him more terrible than ever. He feels that only the love of his wife prevents him from despairing. His doubts never leave him. 'I cannot live without knowing what I am and why I am here,' he would say to himself, 'and that I can't know, so therefore I can't live.' But Levin did not shoot himself, nor did he hang himself. He went on living:

So he lived, not knowing and not seeing any chance of knowing what he was and for what purpose he had been placed in the world. He was tormented by this ignorance to the extent of fearing suicide, yet at the same time he was resolutely cutting his own individual and definite path through life.

Count Vronsky has no such problems. He is handsome and charming, an officer in the army, and in love with the beautiful Anna. His moment of crisis comes when Anna gives birth to their child. Delirious with puerperal fever, Anna seems close to death. Her husband, Karenin, has been contemplating divorce, but now, confronted by her fearful illness, he forgives her. Filled with emotion and the joy of forgiving, he tells Vronsky,

'You may trample me in the mire, make me the laughing stock of the world, I will not forsake her and will never utter a word of reproach to you. . . . My duty is plain to me: I ought to remain with her, and I will. Should she want to see you, I will let you know, but now I think you had better go.'

Vronsky feels there is 'something lofty and inaccessible to him in Karenin's outlook on life' and he is overcome with shame, humiliation and guilt. He finds that he has suddenly exchanged roles with Karenin, who until now has been the pitiful, deceived husband but who is now no longer vindictive, false and ludicrous, but kind, straightforward and dignified. He has a sense of 'Karenin's elevation and his own abasement, Karenin's integrity and his own untruth'. At the very moment when he has come to realize how deeply he loves Anna he feels that he has been humiliated before her, 'leaving with her nothing of himself but a shameful memory'. Returning home he tries to sleep and forget, but he is tormented by the memory of Karenin's words of forgiveness, 'You may trample me in the mire.' Still trying to put the events of the day out of his mind, he hears 'a strange, mad whisper, "You did not appreciate her, you did not make enough of her." ' He asks himself if he is going out of his mind. 'What makes men lose their reason? What makes them shoot themselves?' His mind runs through his life apart from his love for Anna. The things that once had meaning for him — ambition, his friends, society, the court — no longer have. 'This is how people go mad . . . and shoot themselves . . . to escape humiliation.' 'Of course,' he says, repeating this phrase to himself several times. He picks up his revolver and shoots himself in the chest. He does not die, however, but recovers to resume his affair with Anna. His suicide attempt has been an impulsive act after only a few hours' mounting despair at his shame and the thought that there is nothing left for him of all that makes his life worth living.

Anna's story is quite different and, in the way that the idea of suicide develops over a long period, it is perhaps more typical of what happens in real life than is Vronsky's. She is an attractive woman, beautiful, charming and passionate, but she is trapped in a loveless marriage. Her husband is an ambitious man, much concerned with the proprieties demanded by the society they live in. Always courteous to her, he does not, cannot, offer her the warmth she needs. For Anna there is only her love as a mother and she is deeply devoted to her son, Seriozha. We first meet her when she visits her brother in Moscow, and it is there, at the railway station, that she is introduced to the dashing Count Vronsky. While they are at the station there is an accident in which a guard is killed, crushed by a shunting train. 'What a terrible death! They say he was cut in half,' says one gentleman. 'On the contrary, I think it was the easiest of deaths — instantaneous,' remarks another. Anna, clearly upset by the incident, declares that it is a bad omen.

When she returns to Petersburg her relationship with Vronsky develops and they become lovers. She confesses her affair to her husband, who, though disgusted by her adultery, demands that they must continue to present an image of respectability to society. She sees that there is to be no escape from her marriage.

> She knew . . . that everything would go on as it was — would, in fact, be far worse than before. She felt that the position she enjoyed in society, which had seemed of so little consequence that morning, was precious to her after all, and that she would not have the strength to exchange it for the shameful one of a woman who has deserted her husband and child to join her lover; that, however much she might struggle, she could not be stronger than herself. She would never know freedom in love, but would be the guilty wife continually threatened with exposure, deceiving her husband for the sake of a disgraceful liaison with a man living apart and away from her, whose life she could never share. She knew that this was how it would be, and yet it was so awful that she could not even conceive what it would end in.

Later she asks Vronsky to call on her. By now she is pregnant. She tells him, 'Soon — soon everything will come right and we shall all, all be at peace, and suffer no more.' She says that a long time ago she had a strange dream and that when, still dreaming, she asked what it meant she was told that she would die in childbirth. On the following day Karenin, furious that his wife should have had another meeting with Vronsky, exposes his anger and she tells him, 'Soon, very soon, it will come to an end of itself,' and 'at the thought of the nearness of death, which she now longed for', tears fill her eyes. After the birth of her child and her recovery from the fever that follows it her irritability explodes with: 'Oh God, why didn't I die?' As she had predicted, everything is now worse than before, 'I have heard it said that women love men even for their vices', she tells her brother, 'but I hate him [Karenin] for his virtues,' and she goes on:

> 'I can't live with him. Do you understand — the sight of him has a physical effect on me? It puts me beside myself. I can't, I can't live with him. What am I to do? I was unhappy before, and used to think one couldn't be more unhappy but the awful state of things I am going through now, I could never have conceived. Would you believe it — knowing he is a good, excellent man, that I am not worth his little finger, still I hate him! I hate him for his generosity. And there is nothing left for me but . . .'

Her brother stops her before she can utter the word 'death', but she goes on:

> 'I'm lost, lost! Worse than lost! I'm not lost yet — I can't say that all is over: on the contrary, I feel that it's not yet ended. I'm like an over-strained violin string that must snap. But it's not ended yet . . . and the end will be terrible.'

Her brother tries to comfort her, to reassure her that there is no situation from which there is no way out. 'I have thought and thought', she says, 'there is only one . . .' and her brother knows what the unspoken word was.

Attempts are made to persuade Karenin to give his wife a divorce, but he continues to refuse. Anna, who has been told that after her illness further children are out of the question, is ever more distraught and can now sleep only with the help of morphine. Finally she leaves her husband and son to live in the country with Vronsky. As time goes on she begins to feel that his affection for her is beginning to cool and it is only by keeping herself occupied during the day and by taking drugs at night that she can suppress the thought of what would happen if he were to stop loving her. She begins to resent his absences and on one occasion uses the veiled threat, 'How near disaster I am, how afraid of myself,' but she realizes that this is a dangerous weapon that she must not use a second time. Her rows with Vronsky continue and become more bitter. She is convinced that he no longer loves her and indeed life with Anna is becoming more difficult for him. Her parting shot in one of their angriest exchanges is, 'I want your love, and it has gone. So it is all over.' Turning this over in her mind when she is alone, she adds, 'and I must end it.' This particular row is followed by a passionate reconciliation but, almost inevitably, there comes an occasion when there is no reconciliation and, Tolstoy tells us:

> The idea of death presented itself clearly and vividly as the sole means of reviving his love for her, of punishing him and of gaining the victory in the contest which the evil spirit in her heart was waging against him. Nothing mattered to her now . . . it was all useless. The one thing that mattered was to punish him. When she poured out her usual dose of opium and thought that she had only to swallow the whole bottleful to die, it seemed to her so simple and easy that she again knew real enjoyment in imagining how he would suffer, repent, and cherish her memory when it was too late. She lay in bed with wide-open eyes staring at the

light of a single burned-down candle at the moulded cornice of
the ceiling, and the shadow the screen cast on it, while she vividly
pictured to herself what he would feel when she was no more,
when she was nothing but a memory for him. 'How could I have
said those cruel things to her?' he would think. 'How could I have
left the room without a word? But now she is no more. She has
gone from us for ever. She is there . . .' Suddenly the shadow of
the screen wavered, pounced on the whole cornice, the whole
ceiling. Shadows from the other side darted across to meet it. For
an instant they rushed back, then moved up with fresh swiftness,
flickered, blended, and all was darkness. 'Death!' she thought. And
such horror fell upon her that for a long while she could not make
out where she was and her trembling hands could not find a match
with which to light another candle in the place of the one that
had burned low and gone out.

'No, anything — only to live! Why, I love him! And he loves
me! All this was in the past and will go,' she said, feeling tears of
joy at her return to life trickling down her cheeks. And to escape
from her panic she hurried down to his room.

How accurately Tolstoy reveals the illogical and mixed motives
that lead Anna to contemplate suicide. She visualizes the effect
of her death solely in terms of the effect it will have on Vronsky.
But the repentance it might wring from him will be of no benefit
to her. It is as if she somehow imagines that even after killing herself
she will be there to enjoy his contrition. And how convincingly
does Tolstoy show us the changes of mood, the conflict of her
will to live and her urge to die. One moment the thought of suicide
gives her a kind of satisfaction; the next, it fills her with horror.

In the end Anna goes to the railway station. There *is* a way
out for her there, and she takes it, dropping herself in front of
a goods truck. And movingly Tolstoy returns to the imagery of
the flickering candle when he describes her death:

> And the candle by which she had been reading the book filled
> with trouble and deceit, sorrow and evil, flared up with a brighter
> light, illuminating for her everything that before had been
> enshrouded in darkness, flickered, grew dim, and went out for
> ever.

Out, out, brief candle! So skilful is Tolstoy that we can fully
understand how Anna's self-destructive thoughts develop, almost
subconsciously at first, but later surfacing to wage open war on
her will to survive. We can comprehend *why* she eventually brings

her life to an end. She has sacrificed her reputation for a little happiness. She has lost contact with her son. She has been ostracized by the society to which she belonged and in which she had been esteemed for her beauty. She has done all this to be with one man, and when it seems that he might be about to leave her she fears that she will end up with nothing. Although Vronsky has not yet left her she derives no comfort from the conversations she has with him. She is alone, isolated. And she is no longer comfortable with herself. Filled with shame that she has engaged in a 'disgraceful liaison', she has lost the image of herself as the kind of person she and, she believes, others can respect. These are the components of her loneliness and despair, but there is another element of alienation: it is her anger, the desire to punish. This, too, contributes to her final, fatal isolation.

Anna Karenina illustrates a number of points which are relevant to our study. First there is the ambivalence in Anna's thinking; not only does she vacillate between the thought of suicide and the desire to continue living, but in her confused thinking there appears to be some uncertainty about what her intention is. Does she truly wish to die or does she merely wish to punish Vronsky? Then there is the question of motive. We have discerned that all her feelings of loss, all her reasons for dying, amount in the end to isolation; that is the common factor. But from her point of view she has several distinct motives for killing herself. These two features of Anna's story, the ambivalence of her thinking and the multiplicity of her motives seem to have many parallels elsewhere, so we shall now examine them in a little more detail.

We all like to suppose that our decisions are governed by logical thought. After all, is it not reason which distinguishes us humans from the beasts? We must not be surprised, therefore, to find many instances in literature of individuals presenting rational arguments for or against their own suicides. We shall be referring to two of these in Chapter 9 (Kirillov in Dostoevsky's *The Possessed* and Socrates in Plato's *Phaedo*). Such argument is not confined, however, to characters in literature. I have heard the case for suicide argued by supporters of voluntary euthanasia. Often it goes something like this: I am fit and healthy now and enjoy life to the full, but if in the fulness of time my faculties should become impaired I should wish then to end my life. It sounds logical enough: no one would be astonished to learn that Beethoven, realizing that his hearing was failing, gave serious thought to suicide. But such arguments take no account of the feelings of

the individual *at the time*. (We shall return to this point.) Many
people attempt to draw up a kind of balance sheet in which they
seek to compare the pros and cons of living. They see this as
a rational process, but they forget that the premises on which
they base their arguments are all to do with feelings. Shakespeare
put the logical question with marvellous clarity in Hamlet's great
monologue:

> To be, or not to be: that is the question:
> Whether 'tis nobler in the mind to suffer
> The slings and arrows of outrageous fortune,
> Or to take arms against a sea of troubles,
> And by opposing end them?

But the thinking that eventually leads to an answer will be at the
level of feelings. Hamlet continues:

> . . . To die: to sleep;
> No more; and, by a sleep to say we end
> The heart-ache and the thousand natural shocks
> That flesh is heir to, 'tis a consummation
> Devoutly to be wish'd. To die, to sleep;
> To sleep; perchance to dream: ay, there's the rub;
> For in that sleep of death what dreams may come
> When we have shuffled off this mortal coil,
> Must give us pause. There's the respect
> That makes calamity of so long life;
> For who would bear the whips and scorns of time,
> The oppressor's wrong, the proud man's contumely,
> The pangs of dispriz'd love, the law's delay,
> The insolence of office, and the spurns
> That patient merit of the unworthy takes,
> When he himself might his quietus make
> With a bare bodkin? Who would fardels bear,
> To grunt and sweat under a weary life,
> But that the dread of something after death,
> The undiscover'd country from whose bourn
> No traveller returns, puzzles the will,
> And makes us rather bear those ills we have
> Than fly to others that we know not of?
> Thus conscience does make cowards of us all;
> And thus the native hue of resolution
> Is sicklied o'er with the pale cast of thought,
> And enterprises of great pith and moment
> With this regard their currents turn awry,
> And lose the name of action.

Hamlet is not mad. The thoughts and feelings he expresses are those of a man haunted by corruption and plagued by doubts. His circumstances are extreme, but the inner turmoil enshrined in Shakespeare's noble language is no different from the suicidal anguish of ordinary mortals. As C. S. Lewis said, 'I would go a long way to meet Beatrice or Falstaff . . . I would not cross the road to meet Hamlet. It would never be necessary. He is always where I am.'[19]

Ambivalence is a feature of the thinking of most suicidal people. Their attitude towards deliberately terminating their own lives is not constant. There may be long periods when no suicidal thoughts occur. There may be times when there is a conscious inner debate: 'To be, or not to be.' At other times a black mood may prevail and it then seems that no other frame of mind is possible, even though there has been previous experience of similar moods that have passed away. The urge to live may be represented in a variety of forms: the recollection of happier days, an anxiety about the effect of suicide on those who are dear, a revulsion against the act (such as Anna Karenina has as she lies in the candlelight), a fear that one might in a moment of thoughtless passion commit the act (like Levin and his avoidance of ropes and guns), a fear of what might lie beyond death (Hamlet's 'what dreams may come'.), a religion-inspired feeling that suicide is wrong and perhaps many others. Equally, the wish to die can come in various guises: a sense of one's own worthlessness, a feeling of being totally alone and unloved or unwanted, grief, pain, a feeling that nothing lies ahead or can lie ahead, the thought that whatever happens does not matter. The tragedy of suicide is that so often the irrevocable act is committed when the mood is only temporary. I remember having many conversations with a friend who took an overdose when her marriage broke up. She intended to die, wanted to die, but she was found and taken to hospital. When she woke up she was angry to find that her attempt had failed, that someone had interfered, that she was still alive. Later, when I knew her, her life had changed and she was happy and fulfilled. The fact that her survival was an accident is a poignant reminder of the futility of a great many, if not all, suicide attempts. The poet, William Cowper, in his *Needless Alarm*, makes the point clearly:

> Beware of desp'rate steps. The darkest day
> (live till tomorrow) will have passed away.[20]

Or, as Voltaire puts it, 'The man who, in a fit of melancholy, kills himself today, would have wished to live had he waited a week.'[21] Suicide is the ultimate closing of options. It leads nowhere. Sadly, that is precisely where some people want to go. 'Stop the world — I want to get off.'[22]

There is another kind of ambivalence in much suicidal thinking. We naturally think that anyone who takes his own life wishes to be dead, but in fact this is not so; not all suicidal feelings are experienced as a desire to be dead. For many people the total annihilation of death is not what they seek, but rather something more akin to sleep. It is not that they have an intellectual image of death as being some temporary state. It is rather that death is an unavoidable or unconsidered concomitant of the release that the suicidal act is intended to bring. Tennyson felt that:

> Whatever crazy sorrow saith,
> No life that breathes with human breath
> Has ever truly longed for death.[23]

Freud expresses it differently. In his *Thoughts for the Times on War and Death* he writes:

> The psychoanalytic school could venture on the assertion that at bottom no one believes in his own death, or, to put the same thing in another way, that in the unconscious every one of us is convinced of his own immortality.[24]

Keats, in his *Ode to a Nightingale*, expresses the wish:

> That I might drink, and leave the world unseen,
>   And with thee fade away into the forest dim:
> Fade far away, dissolve, and quite forget
>   What thou among the leaves hast never known,
> The weariness, the fever, and the fret
>   Here, where men sit and hear each other groan;
> Where palsy shakes a few, sad, last grey hairs,
>   Where youth grows pale, and spectre-thin, and dies;
> Where but to think is to be full of sorrow
>   And leaden-eyed despair;
> Where Beauty cannot keep her lustrous eyes,
>   Or new Love pine at them beyond tomorrow.

He speaks as though he were tired of life. Is it death he seeks when later in the same poem he says,

> . . . and for many a time
> I have been half in love with easeful Death,
> Call'd him soft names in many a mused rhyme,
> To take into the air my quiet breath;
> Now more than ever seems it rich to die,
> To cease upon the midnight with no pain. . . .'[25]

— or is it release from the pains of living? One cannot be certain, but the emphasis seems to be less on death than on escape, the wish to forget the weariness, the fever and the fret. Robert Graves, in his poem, *The Suicide in the Copse*, says of the victim:

> Had not his purpose been
> To liberate himself from duns and dolts
> By a change of scene?[26]

It is true that poets often speak of death as being desirable or, as Purcell's Dido has it in her great lament, 'death is now a welcome guest'.[27] The Russian poetess, Anna Akhmatova, in her poem, *To Death,* writes:

> You will come anyway — so why not now?
> I am waiting for you — it's very difficult for me.
> I have put out the light and opened the door
> to you, so simple and wonderful.
> Assume any shape you like,
> Burst in as a poison gas shell,
> or creep up like a burglar with a heavy weight,
> or poison me with typhus vapours.[28]

But is it death that these writers really wish? In his long and moving poem, *The City of Dreadful Night,* James Thomson refers to death as the 'friend-foe' and writes that

> We yearn for speedy death in full fruition,
> Dateless oblivion and divine repose.[29]

Divine repose: that seems to sum up what many people want from suicide. It is not that they want to be dead, to be no more, but rather that they wish not to be present to experience their woes. Perhaps many will feel that to seek death when all that is needed, and indeed wanted, is sleep, a sleep that will knit up 'the ravell'd sleave of care', is beyond all reason. And, of course, it *is* unreasonable, but when one is sorely troubled or deeply depressed the distinction between dateless oblivion and divine repose may seem an unimportant one.

Suicidal thinking may be not only illogical, but may verge on a kind of delirium. Let us return to Anna. As she makes her way to the railway station her thoughts are in turmoil. Even now, when the end is near, her dreadful purpose has not yet surfaced in her mind. Impressions succeed one another in her brain. Recollections of all the causes of her misery seethe within her but at the same time she is constantly distracted by what is going on around her.

'If he [Vronsky] does not love me, but treats me kindly and gently out of a sense of *duty*, and what I want is not there — that would be a thousand times worse than having him hate me. It would be hell! And that is just how it is. He has long ceased to love me. And where love ends, hate begins. I don't know these streets at all. How hilly it is — and houses and houses everywhere. . . . And in the houses people, and more people. . . . No end to them, and all hating each other. Suppose I think to myself what it is I want to make me happy. Well? I get a divorce, and Alexei Alexandrovich [Karenin] lets me have Seriozha, and I marry Vronsky.' Thinking of Karenin she immediately saw him before her with extraordinary vividness — the mild, lifeless, faded eyes, the blue veins in his white hands — heard his intonations and the cracking of his finger joints, and remembering the feeling that had once existed between them, and which had also been called love, she shuddered with revulsion. 'Well, I get divorced, and become Vronsky's wife. What then? Will Kitty cease looking at me as she looked at me today? No. And will Seriozha leave off asking and wondering about my two husbands? And is there any new feeling I can imagine between Vronsky and me? Could there be if not happiness, just absence of torment? No, and no again!' she answered herself now without the smallest hesitation. 'Impossible! Life is sundering us, and I am the cause of his unhappiness and he of mine, and there's no altering him or me. Every attempt has been made but the screw has been twisted tight. . . . A beggar-woman with a baby. She thinks she inspires pity. Are we not all flung into the world for no other purpose than to hate each other, and so to torture ourselves and one another? There go some schoolboys, laughing. Seriozha?' she remembered. 'I thought, too, that I loved him, and used to be moved by my own tenderness for him. Yet here I have lived without him. I exchanged him for another love, and did not complain so long as the other love satisfied me.' And she thought with disgust of what she called the 'other love'. The clearness with which she saw her own life now, and everyone else's, gave her a sense of pleasure.[18]

Once seated in a compartment in the train, she hears the inane conversation of a couple sitting opposite her. Her thoughts about them are spiteful. Then she returns to her own situation and the idea of suicide arises clearly in her mind. Hearing one of her companions say that reason has been given to man to enable him to escape from his troubles, she resumes her reflections.

'Yes, I am very troubled, and reason was given man that he might escape his troubles. Therefore I must escape. Why not put out the candle when there's nothing more to see, when everything looks obnoxious? But how? Why did that guard run along the footboard? Why do those young men in the next carriage make such a noise? Why do they talk and laugh? Everything is false and evil — all lies and deceit!'[18]

She leaves the train and walks along the platform. A goods train is approaching and she remembers the man who was killed the day she first met Vronsky, and she knows what she has to do.

'There,' she said to herself, looking in the shadow of the truck at the mixture of sand and coal dust which covered the sleepers. 'There, in the very middle, and I shall punish him and escape from them all and from myself.'[18]

Tolstoy gives a stark account of the last moments and once again he observes that, even at the very final instant, there is a conflict in Anna's mind. Her will to live is not completely extinguished. One is reminded of Irving Berent's argument in his book, *The Algebra of Suicide*.[30] Suicide attempts, he maintains, are often accompanied by rescue fantasies. The suicidal often wish to be saved. Even although the idea of self-destruction may have been in the victim's mind for some time and the suicidal urges are strong, there is likely to be at least a vestige of hope for the future, or at least a trace of the wish that there were some hope for the future. Premeditation does not eliminate ambivalence. The lacerated hands of suicide victims who have thrown themselves into rivers seem to testify to the fact that there have been efforts to abort the attempts. When, in any area of life, one arrives at a decision after a long period of wrestling with a difficult choice it may be possible to feel quite calm. So it may also be with those who have decided to kill themselves and indeed some suicidal people do exhibit an icy determination or cold indifference to their fate. Even then, however, the habit of living can reassert itself. One thinks of Svidrigailov in Dostoevsky's *Crime and Punishment*. He has decided to end his life and has written a note saying that he dies in full possession of his faculties and that no one is to blame for his death. There is no wish to change his mind. And yet only minutes before he goes out into the street to shoot himself we find him seated at a table:

> The revolver and the note-book lay beside him. Some flies woke up and settled on the untouched veal, which was still on the table. He stared at them and at last with his free right hand began trying to catch one. He tried until he was tired, but could not catch it. At last, realizing that he was engaged in this interesting pursuit, he started, got up, and walked resolutely out of the room. A minute later he was in the street.[31]

The ambivalence of the suicidal is often quite clearly revealed when they speak of their feelings of hopelessness. Juxtaposed with expressions of the wish or intention to die today is the voicing of thoughts that imply survival tomorrow. Tolstoy understood it and he shows it to us in his graphic description of Anna Karenina's last moments.

> She wanted to fall half-way between the wheels of the front truck which was drawing level with her. But the red bag which she began to pull from her arm delayed her, and it was too late: the truck had passed. She must wait for the next. A sensation similar to the feeling she always had when bathing, before she took the first plunge, seized her and she crossed herself. The familiar gesture brought back a whole series of memories of when she was a girl, and of her childhood, and suddenly the darkness that had enveloped everything for her lifted, and for an instant life glowed before her with all its past joys. But she did not take her eyes off the wheels of the approaching second truck. And exactly at the moment when the space between the wheels drew level with her she threw aside the red bag and drawing her head down between her shoulders dropped on her hands under the truck, and with a light movement, as though she would rise again at once, sank on to her knees. At the same instant she became horror-struck at what she was doing. 'Where am I? What am I doing? Why?' She tried to get up, to throw herself back; but something huge and relentless struck her on the head and dragged her down on her back. 'God forgive me everything!' she murmured, feeling the impossibility of struggling.[18]

And so she dies, meaning to and yet not meaning to. The struggle has been an unequal one: the will to live must win every round; the urge to die need take only one and the contest is over. Is this not what life is all about? Each day we have to know, to prove, that life is worth living. Happily most of us seem to be able to take for granted that there is a case for living. So too, however, at some stage of their lives have been a great many, if not all, those who are suicidal. We are not born with the urge to die. It comes upon us. Why? What are the reasons? This brings us to the other important aspect of suicide that emerged from our discussion of *Anna Karenina*: the motive. For all the arguments advanced by Durkheim to support his thesis that the cause of suicide is to be found in society and that the private motives of the victims are only triggers it must be said that the individual contemplating how to hasten his end usually has a clear idea of what it is that makes him feel that way. To be sure, some, possibly all, the reasons will have something to do with external circumstances but the feelings they arouse are subjective and, as far as the suicidal individual is concerned, it is these subjective feelings which are crucial in determining the course he decides to take. Unless we are to assume that the individual is not a free agent, has not even partial autonomy, we must accept that the private motives of the suicide are in some way causal.

When 600 people were asked 'Under what circumstances, if any, would you be relatively indifferent to the idea of your own death?' some said that there were no such circumstances and some gave either no answer or an irrelevant one. Fifty-seven per cent of the answers, however, were along the lines of one of the following:

1. loss of, or decline in, capacity resulting from accident, disease or senility;
2. as a result of high achievement, capacity reaches its limit or the desire for further achievement is exhausted;
3. an environment in which desired goals are absent and will probably never exist. [32]

These answers reflect what it is that makes life worth living for the people concerned. One has to question whether indifference to death would in fact be a component of the frame of mind of these people once such circumstances occurred. One might imagine a young, athletic person suggesting that life would no longer be worth the candle if he were confined to a wheelchair. This could be because he could not put himself in the position of someone deprived of the power to walk. In the event he might well wonder how he could ever have thought that life would be unacceptable under these or indeed any circumstances. That would be because a new *raison d'être* had been found, one which did not depend upon mobility.

In another approach to the question of motives an attempt was made to reconstruct from suicide notes the reasons that had led their authors to kill themselves. A great many, 81 per cent, referred to a desire that could not be fulfilled. Several reasons for the frustration of desires were given, including illness, financial troubles and the influence of other people; some blamed themselves. Fifty-nine per cent revealed intolerable inner conditions: 'I can't stand it any more.' Some gave a poor evaluation of themselves: 'I'll always be a misfit'. Thirty-eight per cent referred to the desirability of suicide.[33] Once again it is not possible to draw any hard and fast conclusions from these findings, except perhaps that in many cases there were a multiplicity of reasons for self-destruction. Albert Bayet in his book, *Le Suicide et la Morale*, enumerates the reasons thus:

> Suicides due to the desire to atone, to avoid the disgrace of punishment, to escape illness, suffering, old age, to not survive a loved one: husband, wife, child, friend, master, to prevent or to expunge an outrage, to avoid disgrace, to avoid falling into the hands of an enemy; suicides due to disgust with life, committed on demand. To these let us add: the inclination to astonish, desire to be spoken about, fit of insanity, idiocy.[34]

Halbwachs detected in all these reasons one common feature. This is how he sums it up:

> All the assumed motives of normal suicide, however different they may appear to us, have the same character. They are facts or circumstances, sentiments or thoughts, which isolate man from society. . . . Psychopaths, too, would kill themselves because they are on the periphery of society and can no longer find a point of support anywhere but within themselves.[7]

'It is not loneliness,' he says, 'but the sentiment one suddenly has of being alone which impels one towards suicide.' Tony Lake in his excellent little book, *Loneliness,* describes it as a kind of progressive illness 'which attacks the personality of people through their communication system'.[35] He identifies three stages. In the first, the individual is cut off from the intimacies of human contact. The victim suffers from a lack of tenderness and a sense of belonging. This can develop to the second stage, in which there is a loss of confidence and the victim's behaviour becomes awkward and inhibits contact with others. 'In the third stage', says Dr Lake, 'our ability to give and receive mutual behaviour is so damaged that it will never be repaired again. We become apathetic — unable to feel.' It is at this point, he suggests, that we become convinced that no one cares what happens to us. Under such circumstances the sense of isolation can be lethal.

We have seen how Tolstoy portrays Anna Karenina's growing feelings of being alone. There are many other examples. Gustave Flaubert's Emma Bovary[36] is an emotional woman and like Anna she is trapped in a marriage that does not provide the kind of love she craves. She seems unable to accept life as it is and longs for an exotic, passionate relationship. She is self-centred and envious and has aspirations to live in a style which she can never achieve. She embarks on two extramarital relationships, both of which fail to bring her long-lasting satisfaction. Poor Emma — she seems to be living in a cage of self-interest, from which she cannot escape. When she receives a letter from her lover, Rodolphe, telling her that he is to go away, to be far from her, she rushes to the attic of her house where she can read the letter without being seen by her husband:

> She leaned against the window-frame and read the letter through, hysterical with rage. But the more she tried to fix her thoughts on it, the more confused they became. She seemed to see him, to hear his voice, to be clasping him in her arms; her heart pounded against her ribs like a battering-ram, thudding faster and faster, leaping wildly. She cast her eyes all round her, wishing she could sink into the earth. Why not have done with it? What was to stop her? She was free. She stepped forward and looked down at the pavement.
>
> 'Go on! Go on!' she said to herself.[36]

Her husband arrives at this moment and 'the thought that she had just been saved from death made her almost faint with terror'. Here again we have the ambiguity of intention that characterizes the death of Anna Karenina, and as the story proceeds towards its end we find Emma in a highly confused state of mind. Eventually, her life ever more painful to her, she takes arsenic, cramming the white powder into her mouth, and she dies. The cause? Flaubert tells us that she has never been happy.

> What caused this inadequacy in her life? Why did everything she leaned on instantaneously decay? . . . Oh, if somewhere there were

a being strong and handsome, a valiant heart, passionate and sensitive at once, a poet's spirit in an angel's form, a lyre with strings of steel, sounding sweet-sad epithalamiums to the heavens, then why should she not find that being? Vain dream! There was nothing that was worth going far to get: all was lies! Every smile concealed a yawn of boredom, every joy a misery. Every pleasure brought its surfeit; and the loveliest kisses only left upon your lips a baffled longing for a more intense delight.[36]

Emma's tragedy is that she fails to accept life as it is. And her selfish desires leave no room for the kind of relationship that she dreams of having. She suffers from a kind of self-induced loneliness.

That 'yawn of boredom' referred to by Flaubert conceals a lethal lack of interest in the ordinary things of life. This is what drives Dostoevsky's Svidrigailov to suicide. On his first meeting with the murderer, Raskolnikov, the central character in *Crime and Punishment*, he is quite explicit:

'You know, there's hardly anything I take interest in . . . especially now, I've nothing to do . . . But I confess frankly, I am very much bored.'[31]

His is a bleak view of life. Speaking to Raskolnikov of life after death, he says:

'We always imagine eternity as something beyond our conception, something vast, vast! But why must it be vast? Instead of all that, what if it's one little room, like a bath house in the country, black and grimy and spiders in every corner, and that's all eternity is? I sometimes fancy it like that.'[31]

John Jones refers in his book, *Dostoevsky*,[37] to the author's notebooks, in which there is a comment relating to the character of Svidrigailov: 'NB. Not an *occupied* man.' 'In fact', says Jones, 'nothing binds him to life.' It is a recipe for disaster. It is this boredom, the lack of anything to bind her to life, which Flaubert sees as the worm in Emma Bovary's heart. Her feeling that 'there was nothing that was worth going far to get' is reminiscent of another character in literature, Franz Kafka's strange Fasting Showman.[38] He is a man who spends his days and nights in a cage, eating nothing. He is an attraction for casual onlookers as well as relays of permanent watchers selected by the public to ensure he is not a fake. The longest time he can fast is fixed by the impresario at forty days, which experience has shown to be the longest the public's interest will last. Then the show moves to another area. This practice goes on for several years with short periods of recuperation. Eventually interest in the spectacle flags, and the placards indicating how long the man has been fasting are no longer kept up to date, but he keeps on fasting. He is forgotten until one day the overseer has the attendants poke about in the straw in the cage. They find the fasting showman still alive. He tells the people gathered round that they shouldn't admire his fasting. Asked why they shouldn't, he says, 'Because I have to fast, I can't do anything else . . . because I couldn't find any food I liked. If I had found any, believe me, I should have made no bones about it and stuffed myself like you or anyone else.' It is clear that he intends to continue fasting. He dies and the overseer has him buried and his cage cleaned out. This strange, rather sardonic tale illustrates in an allegorical way how some people distance themselves from life through being unable to live it the way it is. It is as though some essential ingredient of life has been *withheld*.

More often the essential ingredient of life is *withdrawn*. One of the most common reasons for suicidal feelings is that some aspect of life which has come to be regarded as essential becomes unavailable. It seems that many people put all their eggs in one basket. In a highly commendable way they commit themselves to some person or to the attainment of an objective or the maintenance of a certain standard of behaviour. Commitment, however, is not far removed from dependence, and the loss of the object of allegiance can be felt to be the loss of all reason for living. One of the characters in Somerset Maugham's novel, *The Narrow Corner*, puts it quite vehemently:

> 'I'm not prepared to be made a fool of. If life won't fulfil the demands I make on it, then I have no more use for it. It's a dull and stupid play, and it's only waste of time to sit it out. I want life to be fair. I want life to be brave and honest. I want men to be decent and things to come right in the end. That's not asking too much, is it? . . . Resignation? That's the refuge of the beaten. Keep your resignation. I don't want it. I'm not willing to accept evil and injustice and ugliness. I'm not willing to stand by while the good are punished and the wicked go scot free. If life means that virtue is trampled on, and honesty is mocked, and beauty is fouled, then to hell with life.'[39]

'If I can't live life according to my own terms,' the speaker is saying, 'I'd rather be dead.' Expressed thus, it seems an extreme and unreasonable attitude. It is only slightly better than Emma Bovary's, who, we must suspect, would not be happy even if all her dreams were to come true. The expectations are not likely to be realized. Life is *not* fair. As Thackeray says at the end of *Vanity Fair*, 'Which of us is happy in this world? Which of us has his desire, or, having it, is satisfied?'[40] Most of us can accept this sentiment when we are in a period of relative calm and happiness, but when the chips are down it is a different matter. Who can maintain equanimity when his very *raison d'être* is threatened? Whose will to live is not shaken by the loss of a loved one? At such times the demands we have made on life do not strike us as having been unreasonable. Shakespeare's Juliet cannot tolerate the idea of a world that does not contain Romeo. When she finds him poisoned she has no thought but to follow him.

> What's here? a cup, clos'd in my true love's hand?
> Poison, I see, hath been his timeless end.
> O churl! drunk all, and left no friendly drop
> To help me after.

Romeo's suicide is for a similar reason, but there are other motives as well as the loss of Juliet. He dies, as she does, because life without the one he loves is unthinkable, but there is anger too. It is almost as if he were saying, like Maugham's character, 'Then to hell with life.' 'I defy you, stars!' he cries when he is told that Juliet is dead. He is filled with bitterness. As he pays the apothecary who reluctantly and unlawfully has sold him poison, he says:

> There is thy gold, worse poison to men's souls,
> Doing more murders in this loathsome world
> Than these poor compounds that thou mayst not sell:
> I sell thee poison, thou hast sold me none.

There has been much in his short life to give cause for these emotions; insult, banishment, frustration and now the supposed death of Juliet. To all these we must add youth. Bereavement is perhaps the worst trial that anyone has to face, but the young have an added dimension. In his autobiography, *Some Day I'll Find You*,[41] Harry Williams refers to a comment, which he attributes to E. M. Forster. 'Perhaps the worst thing about being young', he says, 'is that you have no experience of disaster survived when, that is, your girl gives you up or everything at the moment is as black as pitch.' Goethe makes the same observation when, recounting the story of a young girl who has been seduced and abandoned, he says:

> Numbed, distracted, she finds herself at the edge of a precipice.

Naught but shadows surround her. No perspective, no consolation, no presentiment. For the only one who made her feel alive has left her. She does not see at all how vast is the world, or the many others in it who could replace what she has lost. She feels herself alone, abandoned by all. The future closes up again before her.[42]

And that phrase, 'The future closes up again before her', describes exactly the feelings experienced by the 19-year-old Esther in Sylvia Plath's novel, *The Bell Jar*.[43]

I saw the years of my life spaced along a road in the form of telephone poles, threaded together by wires. I counted one, two, three . . . nineteen telephone poles, and then the wires dangled into space, and try as I would, I couldn't see a single pole beyond the nineteenth.

We have already seen that one of the many reasons behind Anna Karenina's death was her desire to punish Count Vronsky: 'I will punish him. He'll be sorry when I am no longer here.' This is a way of thinking which seems to be almost as old as man himself. One classic example is in the story of Dido and Aeneas, which was told by the Roman poet, Virgil, in his epic poem, *The Aeneid*. It is a simple tale of love and desertion, but in his description of Dido's rage at her betrayal by Aeneas, Virgil gives us a most credible insight into the part anger can play in providing a powerful motive for suicide. Dido is the Queen of Carthage and Aeneas is her Trojan lover. Their affair is the subject of much rumour, which sweeps through the cities of Libya, 'the swiftest traveller of all the ills on earth':

Item, Aeneas has come here, a prince of Trojan blood,
And the beauteous Dido deigns to have her name linked with his;
The couple are spending the winter in debauchery, the whole long
Winter, forgetting their kingdom, rapt in a trance of lust.
Such gossip did vile Rumour pepper on every mouth.[44]

One can well imagine then that when at last Dido learns that Aeneas plans to leave her she has many reasons for feeling suicidal. First, of course, there is the prospect of life without the man she loves; and so she pleads with him to stay, but he cannot. Then there is the damage that has been done to her image. She tells Aeneas that:

Because of you, the Libyan tribes and the Nomad Chieftains
Hate me, the Tyrians are hostile: because of you I have lost

My old reputation for faithfulness — the one thing that could have
    made me
Immortal.

She is, Virgil tells us, 'frightened out of her wits by her destiny'
and her dreams are of 'unending solitude and desertion, of
walking alone and eternally down a long road, through an empty
land'. It is the fear of isolation — a fear which plays a part in many
suicides — and, indeed, Dido begins to plan her own death. All
her entreaties having failed to persuade Aeneas to stay, she can
see no other course. But it is anger which seems to dominate
her thinking. Her death is at least in part aimed at hurting him,
and in the end she can only curse him:

        Go, sail to your realm overseas!
I only hope that, if the just spirits have any power,
Marooned on some mid-sea rock you may drink the full cup of
    agony
And often cry out for Dido. I'll dog you, from far, with the
    death-fires;
And when cold death has parted my soul from my body, my
    spectre
Will be wherever you are. You shall pay for the evil you've done me.
The tale of your punishment will come to me down in the shades.

Finally, as the Trojan ships carrying Aeneas and his men have
departed but are still within sight of the shore Dido climbs on
to the lofty pyre she has had prepared and using a sword belonging
to Aeneas kills herself. Her last words tell of her anger:

        Shall I die unavenged?
At least, let me die. Thus, thus! I go to the dark, go gladly.
May he look long, from out there on the deep, at my flaming pyre,
The heartless! And may my death-fires signal bad luck for his
    voyage!

Dido's anger at Aeneas has been turned against herself. It is as
if she kills herself as a means of exacting some kind of retribution.
This desire to hurt another person is not an uncommon element
in suicide. 'A suicide kills two people, Maggie, that's what it's for,'
writes Arthur Miller in his play, After the Fall.[45] Like many of the
other motives for suicide this one has a strange illogicality about
it. It seeks the achievement of an end which the victim will not
be able to enjoy. It is possible to savour in the imagination the
effect of the act before it is performed, but the act itself adds
nothing to the appreciation of it.

It is not only in the context of suicide for retribution that this paradox arises. We find it also in suicides directed towards the recovery of self-image. There are several instances in Shakespeare. One of these is Lucrece. She kills herself in the hope that she can recover her lost honour. She has been raped by Tarquinius and, like Hamlet, she wrestles with the question, 'to be or not to be'.

> As the poor frightened deer, that stands at gaze,
> Wildly determining which way to fly,
> Or one encompassed in a winding maze,
> That cannot tread the way out readily;
> So with herself she is at mutiny,
> To live or die which of the twain were better,
> When life is sham'd, and death reproach's debtor.

She has three reasons for killing herself. The first is to escape from the pain of humiliation. The second is to spare her husband the dishonour of having a wife who is no longer chaste. The third is her hope that her own honour will in some sense be recovered and will survive after she is dead:

> For in my death I murder scorn:
> My shame so dead, mine honour is new-born.

Another Shakespearian example of suicide directed at the preservation of self-image comes in Julius Caesar. Brutus, having participated in the assassination of Caesar, becomes increasingly depressed. Not only is his conscience troubling him but he has suffered the loss of his wife, Portia. He confesses to his friend Cassius,

> O Cassius! I am sick of many griefs.

How apt is that phrase, sick of many griefs. It describes the state of mind of many suicidal people. So often there seem to be a whole series of justifications for their desire to end their lives. Although at any one instant only one is uppermost in their thoughts it is almost as if there were a kind of synergism, each reason reinforcing the others. So it is for Brutus, sick of many griefs: but when he dies he reveals what it is that has been preying most upon his mind. It is remorse, the gnawing pain of conscience:

> Caesar, now be still;
> I kill'd not thee with half so good a will.

Is there not in remorse a strong element of loss of self-image, the feeling that one's performance has fallen below the standards one has set for oneself?

We can see a similar motivation in Othello's suicide. To be sure, his grief at the loss of his wife is one of the components of his despair: in murdering Desdemona he

> . . . threw a pearl away
> Richer than all his tribe.

But Othello is a man of great character and we feel that under other circumstances he would have been able to survive his bereavement. Through all his misery, however, runs the thought of his lost self-image. Once a great general, he cannot accept himself as the uxoricidal victim of jealousy. He cannot believe that he has come so low:

> It is the very error of the moon;
> She comes more near the earth than she was wont,
> And makes men mad,

he tells Emilia when she finds him by the smothered Desdemona. He recalls past glories:

> Behold! I have a weapon;
> A better never did itself sustain
> Upon a soldier's thigh: I have seen the day,
> That with this little arm, and this good sword,
> I have made my way through more impediments
> Than twenty times your stop: but O vain boast!
> Who can control his fate? 'tis not so now.

And when he dies it is clear that he does so in the hope that his former reputation will be preserved:

> Soft you; a word or two before you go.
> I have done the state some service, and they know't;
> No more of that. I pray you, in your letters,
> When you shall these unlucky deeds relate,
> Speak of me as I am; nothing extenuate,
> Nor set down aught in malice: then, must you speak
> Of one that lov'd not wisely but too well;
> Of one not easily jealous, but, being wrought,
> Perplex'd in the extreme . . .

It is the same with Antony. He dies because he has lost Cleopatra but also because he has lost his reputation as a great leader and, were he to survive, he would have to face the ignominy of being paraded through Rome as one who has been vanquished. He falls on his sword and as he dies his thoughts are of the days of his greatness.

> The miserable change now at my end
> Lament nor sorrow at; but please your thoughts
> In feeding them with those my former fortunes
> Wherein I liv'd, the greatest prince o' the world,
> The noblest; and do not now basely die,
> Not cowardly put off my helmet to
> My countryman; a Roman by a Roman
> Valiantly vanquished.

And for her part Cleopatra dies for a similar range of reasons. She is to lose Antony, but in taking her own life she is not only responding to her bereavement: she is preserving her reputation as a great queen. She tells Caesar's friend,

> . . . Know, sir, that I
> Will not wait pinion'd at your master's court,
> Nor once be chastis'd with the sober eye
> Of dull Octavia. Shall they hoist me up
> And show me to the shouting varletry
> Of censuring Rome? Rather a ditch in Egypt
> Be gentle grave unto me!

Suicide is now her chosen way;

> The stroke of death is as a lover's pinch,
> Which hurts, and is desir'd,

and she applies an asp to her breast.

Another aspect of self-image is the desire not to sacrifice a principle. Here the preservation of an ideal or a standard of behaviour is considered more important than life itself. Merseult in Albert Camus's novel, *The Outsider*,[46] dies for truth. He does not kill himself, but his refusal to lie is suicidal. He has killed an Arab and is tried for murder. He has no heroic pretensions but because he feels compelled to speak only the absolute truth his case is badly presented and he is found guilty and will be executed. There is a parallel in the behaviour of Desdemona. She does not kill herself, but her acceptance of the risk that Othello will end her life has the same consequence.

> All's one. Good faith! how foolish are our minds!
> If I do die before thee, prithee, shroud me
> In one of those same sheets,

she says to her maid, Emilia, as she prepares for bed. She would rather die than displease Othello or be disloyal to him.

> . . . my love doth so approve him,
> That even his stubbornness, his checks and frowns,
> . . . have grace and favour in them.

And so she dies, smothered by the jealous Moor. Even after Othello's lethal act, as she is dying, she preserves her loyalty. Asked 'Who hath done this deed?' she replies,

> Nobody; I myself; farewell:
> Commend me to my kind lord.

This is an extreme case, but not wholly beyond belief. How many women expose themselves to the risk of severe and possibly fatal injuries by continuing to live with violent husbands? There may be other reasons for their doing so, but many of them when asked, 'Do you love your husband', will answer, possibly after a few moment's thought, that they do.

It seems probable that there is in the stress of work an element of fear of loss of self-image. There are, of course, many factors that contribute to the stresses associated with work. Not least of these are the irritations and pressures in the relationships between the worker and his employer or supervisor. Stress arises if the targets set by the employer, that is his expectations, are seen to be too high or are unattainable, possibly because they are always shifting. Work can become stressful because the employee lacks autonomy; too much autonomy can also put pressure on him. Distress can arise through a conflict in loyalties, for example between duty towards an employer and the calls made by union membership. A sudden change in working conditions can be extremely upsetting because of the real or implied threat of adverse consequences: an increase in work load, a reduction of rewards or privileges, a loss of status or of job security. The routineness and meniality of jobs can cause stress, as can the isolation of a worker, either through the loneliness of his location or by the neglect of his employer and colleagues. Overloading and the resulting fatigue can be hazardous. Some jobs, such as mining, exert special pressures because they are carried out in unpleasant or even hostile environments. In fact miners came at the top of a 'stress league' drawn up by the University of Manchester Institute of Science and Technology.[47] They were closely followed by police, construction workers, journalists, pilots, prison officers, those in advertising, dentists, actors, politicians, doctors, taxmen, film producers, nurses and midwives, firemen, musicians and teachers. The list continued through staff in personnel work, social workers and so on, down to museum workers and librarians at the bottom end of the scale. Company executives, too, are subject to stress. This can result from having too much to do, but guilt is often a basic factor, guilt because a wrong decision has been taken or guilt because of a feeling that, however much is being done, it isn't enough.

Work-induced stress can lead to depression and ultimately to suicide. It is seldom a single crisis that causes death, although some stressful event may be the trigger. As with other factors leading to suicidal thoughts, there is usually an extended build-up during which the job and other circumstances 'get on top of' the person concerned. Quite often close colleagues are totally unaware that trouble is brewing. The victim keeps his problems to himself, and indeed this is often a significant factor in his depressed state: he cannot share his anxieties with anyone. I have known a number of people who have taken their own lives and it is perhaps not very surprising that in several instances colleagues have remarked that 'he was a very private person'. It may be that the person of whom such things can be said has had a secretive or reclusive personality that made it difficult or undesirable for him to share his feelings and problems with anyone. On the other hand he may have felt shame about some perceived deficiency in his performance, or he may have felt that to air his difficulties would be regarded as an inability to handle the job. Whatever the reason, there has been a sense of isolation. The person whose self-image has been lost often assumes that others will perceive him in the same negative way that he sees himself, and so in addition to self-denigration he expects the disapproval of those around him.

Unemployment may be just as stressful as, perhaps much more stressful than, work itself. The threat of redundancy and all the uncertainty it entails is hard to bear and, although the final severance from employment may represent an end to the pains of anticipation, any initial sense of acceptance is likely to be followed by feelings of rejection and even despair. When one reflects upon what people derive from their jobs one can understand something of the loss that unemployment brings. Work provides an income to support self and family. It also confers status on the individual. Part of one's identity is associated with the job one does: 'I'm a company director,' or 'I'm in computers,' might be the answer to the question: 'Who are you?' One's job is almost as intrinsic a part of one's image as is one's name. A job provides a sense of purpose, a feeling of doing something worthwhile. It gives a structure to the day. It is what makes recreation beneficial. A job provides a community; the worker is part of a group. Redundancy removes all this. It undermines self-esteem. It is a kind of bereavement. For some, of course, employment has always remained beyond their grasp. For them it is difficult not to have a sense of hopelessness. They see the future as holding no promise, and perhaps this perception is simply that of realism rather than negativity. Like the redundant they are without all those benefits that work can offer. Few can escape some feeling of isolation. It is as if society has cast them out.

The sense of not belonging to society, of being an outcast, is the lot of many who end up in prison. They have been told that they are not suitable to live among ordinary human beings. In fact it may be that the reason they are in detention is that they have felt unable or unwilling to be members of the community and that this has been reflected in their antisocial and criminal behaviour. It is small wonder then that prisoners, feeling rejected in this way, suffering all the deprivations that prison life enforces on them and possibly finding themselves the victims of persecution by their fellows, are sometimes prone to suicide. Reports of self-destruction, often by hanging, in prisons are not infrequent. It is likely that the situation is at least as bad among those who are released from detention. The return to freedom represents a move back into the circumstances that led to their conviction, and the stigma of imprisonment makes escape to a new life seem improbable. No one knows how many ex-convicts kill themselves, but the number is likely to be significant.

Acute and chronic distress in any form can provide the reason for suicide. The circumstances of life may become so intolerable that suicide seems less repugnant than continued suffering. The pain may be physical or spiritual or, as in the case of Gloucester in *King Lear*, both. Like Lear himself, Gloucester has renounced the child who loves him and has elected to trust the one who will let him down. Cut adrift from the physical and human comforts of life, cruelly blinded, he is found wandering with Lear

on a lonely heath near Beachy Head. His plight is now unbearable
and he speaks thus to his son Edgar:

> There is a cliff, whose high and bending head
> Looks fearfully in the confined deep;
> Bring me but to the very brim of it,
> And I'll repair the misery thou dost bear
> With something rich about me; from that place
> I shall no leading need.

Brought to what he thinks is Beachy Head, the old man cries,

> O you mighty gods!
> This world I do renounce, and, in your sights,
> Shake patiently my great affliction off;
> If I could bear it longer, and not fall
> To quarrel with your great opposeless wills,
> My snuff and loathed part of nature should
> Burn itself out,

and falls forward, only to strike the ground at his feet. Then he
finds it in himself to say,

> . . . henceforth I'll bear
> Affliction till it do cry out itself
> 'Enough, enough,' and die.

Many elderly people suffering the pains and infirmities of old
age must from time to time wish to renounce the world and, like
Gloucester, shake patiently their great afflictions off. The same
is true for many of those who are terminally ill and who see no
hope of recovery or remission. Their attention becomes enfettered
by the tyranny of their suffering and thus to their physical
tribulations and to their depression must be added their isolation
from those around them.

Spiritual distress has already been exemplified in the thoughts
of Tolstoy's Levin, whose loss of faith caused him so much
torment. Tolstoy himself went through periods of what he called
'arrest'. These moments of perplexity began to occur when he
had reached the age of about 50 and they were characterized by
a feeling that what had once been meaningful was now devoid
of meaning. He was beset by questions about the future. The
following excerpts from his writing reveal the extent to which
Tolstoy put himself into the character of Levin.

I felt that something had broken within me on which my life had always rested, that I had nothing left to hold on to, and that morally my life had stopped. An invincible force impelled me to get rid of my existence, in one way or another. It cannot be said exactly that I *wished* to kill myself, for the force which drew me away from life was fuller, more powerful, more general than any mere desire. It was a force like my old aspiration to live, only it impelled me in the opposite direction. It was an aspiration of my whole being to get out of life.

Behold me then, a man happy and in good health, hiding the rope in order not to hang myself to the rafters of the room where every night I went to sleep alone; behold me no longer going shooting, lest I should yield to the too easy temptation of putting an end to myself with my gun.

I did not know what I wanted. I was afraid of life; I was driven to leave it; and in spite of that I still hoped something from it. . . . What will be the outcome of what I do today? Of what I shall do tomorrow? What will be the outcome of my life? Why should I live? Why should I do anything? Is there in life any purpose which the inevitable death which awaits me does not undo and destroy?

'But perhaps,' I often said to myself, 'there may be something I have failed to notice or to comprehend. It is not possible that this condition of despair should be natural to mankind.' And I sought for an explanation in all the branches of knowledge acquired by men. . . .

Yet, whilst my intellect was working, something else in me was working too, and kept me from the deed — a consciousness of life, as I may call it, which was like a force that obliged my mind to fix itself in another direction and draw me out of my situation of despair. . . . During the whole course of this year, when I almost unceasingly kept asking myself how to end the business, whether by the rope or by the bullet, during all that time, alongside of all those movements of my ideas and observations, my heart kept languishing with another pining emotion. I can call this by no other name than that of a thirst for God. . . . It was like a feeling of dread that made me seem like an orphan and isolated in the midst of all these things that were so foreign. And this feeling of dread was mitigated by the hope of finding the assistance of some one.[48]

Such feelings do not necessarily have to have a religious context. The uncertainties about the nature of one's existence can arise among those whose philosophy of life is purely secular. Arthur Adamov, who came under the influence of the existentialist philosophy of Jean-Paul Sartre, wrote:

What is there? I know first of all that I am. But who am I? All I know of myself is that I suffer. And if I suffer it is because, at the origin of myself, there is mutilation and separation.[49]

Adamov suffered from bouts of depression aggravated by alcoholism. He committed suicide in 1970.

It is interesting that in the examples quoted above the words 'isolated' (Tolstoy) and 'separated' (Adamov) are used. It is as if, whatever the circumstances and the other emotions that come into play, there is a realization that when one examines the depths of one's feelings it is felt that the root of suicidal despair is a sense of isolation. It really does seem that, as Halbwachs suggested, 'All the assumed motives of normal suicide . . . are facts or circumstances, sentiments or thoughts, which isolate man from society.'[7] Nadezhda Mandelstam in her moving memoir, *Hope Against Hope*, writes of her husband, Osip Mandelstam, (referred to as 'M') who suffered under Stalin's regime:

> Like Akhmatova, M. did not believe in suicide in the ordinary sense — even though everything was driving us to it: our loneliness, isolation, and the times themselves, which were scarcely on our side. Loneliness is not just the absence of friends and acquaintances — there are always enough of these — it is rather life in a society which heedlessly, with blindfolded eyes, follows its fratricidal path, dragging everybody with it.[50]

Durkheim would have recognized these sentiments.

One motive for suicide seems to differ from the others: it is altruism. In his novel, *Jude the Obscure*,[51] Thomas Hardy paints a touching and melancholy picture of a child who takes his own life for altruistic reasons. In the following excerpt we find the child in conversation with Sue, who is living with his father, Jude.

> ''Tis because of us children, too, isn't it, that you can't get a good lodging?'
> 'Well people do object to children sometimes.'
> 'Then if children make so much trouble, why do people have 'em?'
> 'O — because it is a law of nature.'
> 'But we don't ask to be born?'
> 'No indeed.' . . .
> 'I think that whenever children be born that are not wanted they should be killed directly, before their souls come to 'em, and not allowed to grow big and walk about!'
> Sue did not reply. She was doubtfully pondering how to treat this too reflective child.
> She at last concluded that, so far as circumstances permitted,

she would be honest and candid with one who entered into her difficulties like an aged friend.

'There is going to be another in our family soon,' she hesitatingly remarked.

'How?'

'There is going to be another baby.'

'What!' The boy jumped up wildly. 'O God, mother, you've never a-sent for another; and such trouble with what you've got!'

. . .

He got up, and went away into the closet adjoining her room, in which a bed had been spread on the floor. There she heard him say:

'If we children was gone there'd be no trouble at all!'

'Don't think that, dear,' she cried, rather peremptorily. 'But go to sleep.'

The next morning the horrified parents find all their children dead. They have been hanged, including the elder boy, little Jude. A piece of paper is found upon the floor. On it, written in the boy's hand are the words: 'Done because we are too menny.' This appears to be an act stemming from love of the family of which little Jude is a part. Yet there is an element of isolation, of separation. He sees his family as an entity that need not, and ultimately does not, include him. He cannot feel that he is an essential part of the unit. He is not aware that his selfless act destroys what he would preserve.

Before we leave the subject of motive we must consider one other kind of isolation: that of the person who, because he is in some way different from other men, is rejected by them. Consider, for example, the central character in Dostoevsky's story, *The Dream of a Queer Fellow.*[52] 'I am a queer fellow', the story begins. Dostoevsky offers a pathetic portrait of his character.

I was always queer; perhaps I've known it from the day of my birth. Perhaps when I was only seven I knew that I was queer. Afterwards I went to school, then to the university, and — well, the more I studied the more I discovered that I was queer. . . . Everybody always laughed at me. But not one of them knew or guessed that if there was a man on earth who really knew how queer I was, that man was myself; their not knowing that was quite the most insulting thing of all, but there I was to blame. I was always so proud that nothing would induce me to confess that to anyone.

The queer fellow eventually develops a terrible anguish that 'it would be all the same' to him 'if the world really existed, or if there was nothing anywhere.' The phrase, 'it is all the same,' becomes an obsession and one night he decides to kill himself.

> . . . from the early evening I had been sitting with an engineer I knew, who had two other friends with him. I was silent all the while, and I believe I bored them. They talked of something provocative and suddenly they became quite excited. But it was really all the same to them. I saw that. They were excited all for nothing. Suddenly I broke out: 'I say, gentlemen, . . . but it's all the same to you.' They were not offended, but they all began to laugh at me. . . . While I was thinking about the gas in the street, I glanced at the sky. The sky was terribly black, but I could clearly distinguish the ragged clouds, and between them bottomless spaces of black. Suddenly I caught sight of a little star in one of those spaces and began to stare at it. For the little star had given me an idea: I proposed to kill myself that night. I had firmly decided to kill myself two months before, and though I was very poor, I bought myself an excellent revolver and loaded it that very same day.

The especially touching feature of this portrait is that the man is *aware* that he is not like other people. I am sure that we have all come across queer fellows. Perhaps some of them knew they were queer. Perhaps they were suicidal. If they were it would in all probability be because of their sense of being different, if only in some small and truly unimportant way. Above all it would be because they felt isolated from the warm human contact they saw being shared by those around them.

However one regards the motives for suicide — whether one sees each as being distinct from the others or senses that underlying them all is a common feeling of isolation or loneliness — one is bound to ask why it is that circumstances that drive one person to kill himself are resisted and survived by another. There are many instances of people being subjected to the most appalling deprivations and isolation, not only from those they love but, in some cases, from *all* human contact. One can find examples in the writings of Alexander Solzhenitsyn, such as his harrowing account of Soviet prisons and labour camps in *The Gulag Archipelago*,[53] and other victims of Stalin's tyranny, notably Evgenia S. Ginsburg in her book, *Into the Whirlwind*.[54] Similar atrocities are to be found in the writings of victims of the Holocaust. To us who have never experienced the barbarities of Auschwitz, it may seem remarkable that suicide was not much more common than it in fact was. Viktor Frankl in his book, *Man's*

Search for Meaning,[55] recalls that 'the thought of suicide was entertained by nearly everyone, if only for a brief time.' 'It was', he writes, 'born of the hopelessness of the situation, the constant danger of death looming over us daily and hourly, and the closeness of the deaths suffered by many of the others.' The means were readily available: one had only to run into the electrified wire fence surrounding the camp. Yet those who did so were a minority. One reason offered by Frankl was that 'there was little point in committing suicide, since, for the average inmate, life expectation, calculating objectively and counting all likely chances, was very poor.' There must have been other reasons. Fear of dying, however was not one. 'The prisoner of Auschwitz, in the first phase of shock, did not fear death', says Frankl. 'Even the gas chambers lost their horrors for him after the first few days.' One is reminded of Dostoesvky's novel, *Notes from a Dead House*.[56] Having himself spent four years in the Omsk prison, his description of the conditions under which the convicts in his story live is first-hand.

> When darkness fell, we had to re-enter our barracks to be shut up for the night. I always found it painful to leave the yard for the long, low room dimly lighted by tallow candles and charged with oppressive odours. I can hardly understand how I could have lived there for ten years. My bed was three planks on the bunk shelf; that was all the privacy I had. More than thirty were crowded together on this shelf. We were shut in early in the winter time and there was at least four hours to go before all were asleep. Until then there was a noise, uproar, laughter, oaths, rattling of chains, a poisonous vapour of thick smoke, a confusion of shaven heads, branded foreheads, and ragged clothes, the fallen and the accursed. . . . Yes, a man is hard to die. He is a being who can get used to anything. And that, probably, is the best definition of him.

Viktor Frankl says that if someone were now to ask whether Dostoevsky's statement is correct the reply would be: 'Yes, a man can get used to anything, but do not ask us how.' Frankl quotes Nietsche's words: 'He who has a *why* to live for can bear with almost any *how*.' Perhaps this is as near as we can get to an answer to our question. Frankl suggests that this could be 'the guiding motto' for all psychotherapeutic efforts regarding prisoners.

> Whenever there was an opportunity for it, one had to give them a why — an aim — for their lives, in order to strengthen them

to bear the terrible *how* of their existence. Woe to him who saw no more sense in his life, no aim, no purpose, and therefore no point in carrying on. He was soon lost. The typical reply with which such a man rejected all encouraging arguments was, 'I have nothing to expect from life any more.' What sort of answer can one give to that?

What was really needed was a fundamental change in our attitude towards life. We had to learn ourselves and, furthermore, we had to teach the despairing men, that *it did not really matter what we expected from life, but rather what life expected from us.* We needed to stop asking about the meaning of life, and instead to think of ourselves as those who were being questioned by life — daily and hourly. Our answer must consist, not in talk and meditation, but in right action and in right conduct. Life ultimately means taking the responsibility to find the right answers to its problems and to fulfil the tasks which it constantly sets for each individual.

These are challenging words, probably too challenging for someone suffering from suicidal depression. And yet they describe exactly what Levin did. Remember Tolstoy's comment. Levin was tormented by his ignorance of the purpose of his life, 'yet at the same time he was resolutely cutting his own individual and definite path through life' — which was what Tolstoy himself was doing.

It is probably too much to ask of a suicidal person that he follows this path. The words, the idea, may be prophylactic; they are unlikely to be therapeutic. How would they be received by the man who wrote the following in a letter to the Editor of *The Literary Review?* [57]

A while ago I tried to kill myself in the most fool-proof way I could think of. . . . Nothing happened.

At the time when I did this I was in a frame of mind when I could not feel any love for anyone or get any pleasure from people who loved me.

Because of this there was *nothing whatsoever* that anyone could have said or done to show how much I mattered to them as I would not have believed them. As no one mattered to me, how could I?

These are chilling words. They express the outlook of one who, for a time at least, has lost the *why* of his life. It would have been of little avail to have asked him what he might contribute to life. In his view the only way to prevent the suicide of those who feel as he did would be to lock them up 'so that they have time to change their mind — or just so that time passes'.

It may be that some of us expect too much from life, like the Somerset Maugham character whose words have already been quoted. We have to accept that there will be bad and difficult times for us. Viktor Frankl refers to the poet, Rilke's, way of speaking of 'getting through suffering' as others would talk of getting through work. Frankl says:

> When a man finds that it is his destiny to suffer, he will have to accept his suffering as his task; his single and unique task. He will have to acknowledge the fact that even in suffering he is unique and alone in the universe. No one can relieve him of his suffering or suffer in his place. His unique opportunity lies in the way in which he bears his burden. [55]

It seems that what Frankl is saying is that at times it may be that the *why* in our lives has to be 'getting through suffering'. What can he, or anyone, say to the man who cries out, 'I can't take any more; I can't face tomorrow,' to the person whose *why* has been overwhelmed by all that is intolerable and insuperable in his life? We shall return to this question in Chapters 10 and 11, but for the present let us consider briefly the way in which people find their *why*'s.

Viktor Frankl spoke of giving the prisoners in Auschwitz a *why*, an aim for their lives. It was a matter of giving them mental courage, an ability to stand back and see that their present adversity could be transient and that there was a future to which they could look forward. To put it at its most basic: it amounts to giving them a will to live. I wonder, however, if one can ever *give* someone a will to live. Is it not something which grows within or which has always been there? I may derive my will to live from those around me; they may nourish it, but it is mine. It may come from some religious belief, a conviction that my life has meaning. But what is meaning? It is not something which we can find in nature, in the world around us. It is to be found only in ourselves. 'Meanings', said W. Macneile Dixon, 'are the exclusive property of conscious selves and continuing selves.' [58] Perhaps we have some recollection from the past that sustains us. In his sermon at the stone Dostoevsky's Alyosha Karamazov says:

> . . . there's nothing higher, stronger, more wholesome and more useful in life than some good memory, especially when it goes back to the days of your childhood, to the days of your life at home . . . If a man carries many such memories into life with him, he is saved for the rest of his days. And even if only one good memory

is left in our hearts, it may also be the instrument of our salvation one day.[59]

But the why's that most of us carry in our hearts are not always capable of being defined. They are rooted in, or are the roots of, an attitude that we have grown up with, the perspective from which we view life. It is not a question of logic:

> The most pessimistic of authors, those who cursed life and invoked death as the sole liberator, showed a clean pair of heels whenever they caught sight of it. Leopardi fled from Naples when the cholera broke out. Montaigne vanished from Bordeaux like lightning before the plague. And Schopenhauer would never hear death mentioned, after clearly demonstrating in all his books that life is an evil and death our only boon.[60]

What is it that kept them going in spite of all the reasons they gave for cessation? What unspoken *why* contradicted their fluently articulated arguments? Some people seem, no matter what befalls them, to carry on undaunted like Ol' Man River in the popular song;

> I get weary and sick of tryin';
> I'm tired of livin'
> And scared of dyin',
> But Ol' Man River,
> He jus' keeps rollin' along.[61]

The old fisherman in Ernest Hemingway's story, *The Old Man and the Sea*,[62] exemplifies the survivor. Thin, gaunt and wrinkled, he takes his skiff out into the Gulf Stream each day. For several weeks he has caught nothing and now he has had to go out alone because his boy, receiving no payment, has had to seek work elsewhere. Then one day the old man hooks a giant marlin. All afternoon and through the night he battles with his powerful catch. He tires but persists, all the while talking to himself. In the morning he is still grasping the line. 'You're feeling it now, fish', he says. 'And so, God knows, am I.' All the next day and through the second night the old man holds on, his gnarled hands bleeding and knotted with cramp. When the sun rises again the marlin is weakening and later in the day the old man kills his fish and lashes its carcase to the boat. Exhausted but triumphant he heads for home. Soon after, the sharks come and a new struggle begins. Lashing his knife to an oar, the old man tries to fight off the sharks, but he cannot win this battle. Eventually his fine prize is stripped of its flesh and there is nothing left of it but the great skeleton to show how big it has been. He sails into the little harbour. The town is asleep. He pulls the boat as far out of the water as he can and furls its sail. Putting the mast to his shoulder he sets off to climb slowly to his shack on the hillside. All his strength has gone and when he reaches his home he falls asleep immediately. We know that he will sail again. The story is allegorical and Hemingway states his theme succinctly. 'But man is not made for defeat', the old man says as his fight with the sharks approaches its inevitable conclusion. 'A man can be destroyed but not defeated.'

The old man has a *why*, but would he be able to say what it is? It is enough for him that he knows he must go on to the end. But the *why's* that people have can be unreliable and insecure. There came a time when Hemingway no longer had a *why*. Nine years after writing *The Old Man and the Sea* he shot himself. It is said that he had been tormented by the fact that towards the end of his days he had been finding it increasingly difficult to write and that the outdoor life, which was so much a part of him, had become more and more restricted. Was loss of self-image the motive? Perhaps, but who can tell? The worm, as Camus said, is in man's heart.[2]

4.

THE WARNING SIGNS

There's no art
To find the mind's construction in the face.

Shakespeare, *Macbeth*

When we learn that someone we know has taken his own life our feelings of grief and horror are usually accompanied by shock. Suicide is seldom anticipated. And yet, as has already been observed, it is rare for determined self-destructive action to be an impulse that has not been preceded by suicidal thoughts and urges over a period of days or longer. After the event we may ask ourselves whether preventive measures could have been taken. Had we known what was in the victim's mind might we not have done something? The action which might have been taken is the subject of a later chapter; what we are concerned with here is the possibility of discerning whether there is a risk of suicide, the possibility of knowing, in fact, what is going on in another person's mind. Before attempting to answer that question it might be useful to consider how the individual is likely to be affected by the inner turmoil that leads to his self-inflicted death.

Edwin Shneidman, Professor of Thanatology at the University of California, has likened the suicidal act to an explosion.[63] Just as an explosive has several ingredients and its detonation has to be sparked off in some way, for example by the application of heat, so there are several elements in suicide and there is a single triggering process. Shneidman identifies three elements, which he labels *inimicality, perturbation* and *constriction*. The first of these is a pattern of behaviour in which the individual can be said to be acting in a way that is inimical, or unfriendly, to himself. In other words, his actions are contrary to his own best interests. Among the many ways in which this inimicality can be expressed are the excessive use of alcohol and drugs and the adoption of a destructive approach towards personal relationships with family, friends and colleagues. The danger sign is when such behaviour is heightened and the individual exceeds the normal limits of his indulgence in those activities which are damaging to his prospects of future happiness. It is almost as if he hates himself. Once again we can only wonder at the perceptiveness of Tolstoy, for in *Anna Karenina* he presents clear evidence of Anna's *inimicality*. Her harshest critics, who would include Karenin himself, would no doubt have claimed that her liaison with Count Vronksy was imprudent from the start, but to suggest that it exemplifies the inimicality to which Shneidman refers would be highly doubtful. There is no doubt, however, that the way in which, during her last few days, Anna seems to provoke rows with Vronsky, as if to induce the very estrangement she fears, is the kind of behaviour Shneidman has in mind. She acts as though she were, to quote Shneidman's phrase, her 'own worst enemy'. Her self-hatred emerges when she tells Vronsky that she is 'a wanton, a millstone round [his] neck,' and he is driven to cry, 'Anna, why will you torture yourself and me like this?'[18]

Shneidman's second component, *perturbation*, is the state of 'increased psychological disturbance in the person's life'. It is the extent to which the individual is mentally upset. He may be unusually agitated or worried. Shneidman refers to Henry A. Murray's analysis of the emotional states of men who committed suicide in Veterans' Administration hospitals.[64] These included forlornness and grief, anger and aggression, remorse and depression. Some exhibited leaving or desertion behaviour and others showed no emotional response at all, as if, to use Murray's phrase, they were 'dead to the world'. Once again it is possible to cite Anna Karenina. There is no mistaking her perturbation in the closing pages of the book. Her family can see that all is not well. As she leaves the two sisters, Dolly and Kitty, after calling on them one afternoon they are filled with concern for her.

> 'She's just the same, and as attractive as ever. How beautiful she is!' Kitty said when Anna had gone. 'But there is something pitiful about her, terribly pitiful.'
> 'Yes, there's something peculiar about her today,' said Dolly. 'When I was seeing her out, I fancied she was almost crying.'

Perhaps Shakespeare's Duncan is right; it isn't possible to find the mind's construction from the face, to know what thoughts are there in another mind, but like Tolstoy's Dolly and Kitty we may often be able to guess that something is amiss.

The third of Shneidman's three elements, *constriction*, is also portrayed by Tolstoy. Seated in the train on her way to the station where she ends her life, Anna continues the current of the thoughts that has been flowing through her mind.

> 'Where was it I left off? On the reflection that I couldn't conceive a situation in which life would not be a misery, that we were all created in order to suffer, and that we all know this and all try to invent means for deceiving ourselves. But when you see the truth, what are you to do?'[18]

Anna is revealing *constriction* here. It is a 'narrowing of the range of perception, of opinions and of options that occur to the mind'. Anna can perceive only that there will be misery and that we *all* know this to be the only way things can be. None of the memories and relationships that would normally influence her thinking are now available to her. It is a kind of tunnel vision. Her attention is completely focused on her present painful emotions. An important characteristic of *constriction*, says Shneidman, is:

> a tendency to 'either/or' thinking. The world is divided into two (and only two) parts — good *or* bad, love or hate, a desired life or a 'necessary' death. Such dichotomous thinking in the suicidal person is characterized by words like 'always', 'never', 'forever', 'either/or', and especially the word 'only'.[63]

'There is nothing to be proud of,' reflects Anna as she reviews her affair with Vronsky, '— nothing to be proud of, *only* ashamed.'[18] The tendency to 'either/or' thinking is also there. Retiring to her room after having left word for Vronsky that she has a headache, Anna says to herself,

> If he comes in spite of the maid's message, it means that he loves me still. If he doesn't, it means that all is over, and then I shall have to decide what to do . . .[18]

'When the mind constricts,' writes Shneidman, 'the anguished person sees only the mechanism for stopping the anguish — and that leads to the triggering process.'[63] It is the idea of *cessation*, he suggests, which is the trigger. Stop the world — I want to get off.

> The idea of cessation — that you can be free of all your problems,

get out of this mess, cancel your debts, release yourself from this
anguish, stop this disease — is the turning point in the suicide
drama,[63]

writes Shneidman. And it is the idea of escape that brings to the
surface all Anna's thoughts of death. 'Reason has been given to
man to enable him to escape from his troubles,' says one of her
companions on her last train journey. The words are not addressed
to Anna, but they are the turning point in her drama.

Let us return now to the question with which this chapter
began: can we discern from an individual's behaviour whether
there is a risk of suicide? Regrettably the idea of cessation is often
kept secret. We may become aware that someone is in despair,
and we may even have an inkling that there have been thoughts
of suicide, but the fact that the trigger point has been reached
and that a *plan* for self-destruction is forming in the victim's mind
is likely to be withheld from us. The reason for this secretiveness
is not hard to guess. To speak of suicide as a hypothetical possibility
is one thing; to reveal real intention is quite another. As Shneidman
has pointed out, the idea of cessation is often not communicated
because it is 'so dramatic and so breathtaking and so dangerous'.[64]
The victim may need help in articulating such thoughts. We shall
comment further on this aspect in Chapter 10; for the present
we are concerned with the warning signs that are offered or
inadvertently given.

From what has already been said about inimicality it follows
that any evidence of this pattern of behaviour should be taken
seriously. It is the nature of some people that their relationships
are fraught with their ineptness and a general inability to be on
the wavelength that those around them are on. But when such
behaviour seems deliberate or is clearly on the increase we might
reasonably suspect that it comes into the category referred to by
Shneidman. The same may be true of undue, possibly intentional
carelessness over personal health and safety. Abuse of alcohol
or drugs, especially to the point of dependence, may also be a
danger sign.

The evidence for perturbation may be more immediately
obvious. It may be an unusually high level of aggressiveness or
anger, or it may be anxiety or depression. Long-term disturbance
of sleep is another pointer, especially when the person involved
tends to awaken early in the morning with his mind in turmoil.
(More will be said about this in the chapter on Depression.) We

should also be alerted by a person's inability to relate to us. This might manifest itself as a tendency to appear withdrawn, offering no emotional response, 'dead to the world'. The third element, constriction, might be discernible from conversation. References to suicide, either direct or indirect, should never be ignored. Nor should evidence that someone is 'putting his affairs in order' or getting rid of his possessions. It may seem strange that anyone who has reached the trigger point of contemplating cessation and planning his demise should be concerned with the affairs of the world he intends to leave. But, in fact, it is not uncommon for those about to take their own lives to set things aright before doing so. This may especially be the case with the elderly who are tired of life, of loneliness and of physical suffering. One recalls Carson McCullers' character, the deaf mute, John Singer, washing his ashtray and glass before shooting himself. [65]

There are a number of other factors that contribute to the likelihood that a person might become suicidal. Not least of these is a family history of suicide. There is, it appears, an increased probability of suicide in children who have lost parents through suicide. Professor J. P. Watson has suggested one possible explanation as being in terms of 'parental suicide giving the child an early experience of personal loss and thereby creating vulnerability to subsequent loss experiences' but he recognizes that this explanation might be extended to include other personal losses not involving suicide. [66]

Another factor which must not be ignored when we are assessing the likelihood that an individual might be suicidal is the occurrence of previous attempts. As we shall see when we consider parasuicide, a history of repeated attempts is not infrequently associated with a need for psychiatric treatment. There is a higher likelihood of such persons eventually killing themselves than is found in the rest of the population.

The presence of certain adverse circumstances must also be taken into account. People who are isolated or lonely or who have been uprooted from a supportive background or who have suffered a loss of personal contact, either through bereavement or the disintegration of a relationship, are vulnerable. So, too, are those who are under acute or chronic stress in their jobs or because of financial worries.

Several attempts have been made to construct 'lethality scoring systems' to help to identify those who are most likely to be at risk. One of these, intended for use by those working with possibly suicidal people, depends upon the allocation of points to a series of factors, including a number of those described in this chapter. (See Table 6.) The chief advantages of this system are that it is simple and its use alerts the counsellor to the presence of hazards which might not be immediately obvious. How often have I spoken to someone and concluded that, although there was evidence of suicidal thoughts, there was no real risk; but when I reviewed the circumstances of the person's life in the context of the lethality scoring system I realized just how much pressure was there and how easy it would be for a triggering process to be disastrous.

Another, more complex scale for the assessment of suicide potentiality has been devised by Professor Allen O. Battle, who is Professor of clinical psychology at the University of Tennessee.[67] It includes and distinguishes between factors which are contra-indicative of suicide, such as the feeling that one can still cope, and those which are mildly, moderately and severely lethal. As with the simpler system already described, Professor Battle's scale gives a useful but by no means precise measure of the likelihood that someone will take his own life. Its real value is the help it gives an interviewer to cover a wide spectrum of factors which can lead to suicide. In other words, it is a checklist.

'There is no medical man,' writes Professor Stengel, 'who has never misjudged the risk of suicide in a depressed patient.'[68] Professor Stengel then goes on to list the criteria which psychiatrists have used:

1. Depression with guilt feelings, self-depreciation, and self-accusations, associated with tension and agitation;
2. severe hypochondriasis, i.e. a tendency to continuous complaining, usually about physical symptoms;
3. sleeplessness with great concern about it;
4. fear of losing control, or of hurting others or oneself;
5. previous suicidal attempt;
6. suicidal preoccupation and talk;
7. unsympathetic attitude of the relatives, or life in social isolation;
8. suicides in the family;
9. history of a broken home before the age of 15;
10. serious physical illness;
11. alcohol or drug addiction (the relative frequency of drug addiction among doctors is probably one of the reasons why

suicide is more common among them than in a comparable group of the general population);

12. towards the end of a period of depressive illness, when the depressive mood still persists, but initiative is returning, the risk of suicide is particularly high;

13. dreams of catastrophes, falls, and self-destruction are, according to Professor Kielholz of Basle, indicative of increased suicidal risk if they occur in depressed patients;

14. unemployment and financial difficulties.

In conclusion, let us agree that we cannot prevent suicide. Nor can we read the mind of the suicidal person. But let us recognize also that the majority of those who kill themselves give prior notice of their suicidal feelings. The signs they offer are not always direct allusions to suicide, but they are often sufficiently explicit to enable us to be wise after the event. Sensitivity in those around the potential victim — family, friends and colleagues — can help to detect these signs while it is still possible for help to be given.

5.

DEPRESSION

I hug my pillow and do not speak a word;
In my empty room no sound stirs.
Who knows that, all day a-bed,
I am not ill and am not even asleep?

Po Chü-I, *Poem in Depression, at Wei Village*
(translated by Arthur Waley)

A significant proportion of suicides are the result of mental disorder. Professor Stengel quotes a study made in London in 1955 which suggested that mental disorder was the principal causative factor in 37 per cent of 390 instances of suicide examined and that it was a contributory factor in 47 per cent of the cases.[68] A more recent study referred to in a report published by the Government Statistical Service[10] considered a group of 1,528 psychiatric in-patients admitted for alcoholism in 1964. There were 376 deaths up to the end of 1973. Of these, 26 were suicides, which represents a very much higher proportion than would have been expected in the population at large, for which the figure predicted would have been one. Moreover there was in the group studied an excessive incidence of deaths attributed to accidents, many of which could in fact have been suicides.

There is, of course, a problem of definition. There are those who would regard suicidal behaviour as a clear indication of mental disorder. In other words only those who are mentally disturbed take their own lives. This is certainly not the general view. From his study of the statistics for suicide, mental illness and alcoholism Halbwachs was able to conclude: 'Neither the statistics of insanity nor the statistics of alcohol . . . prove that the majority, or even a very large number, of people who kill themselves are insane or drunks.'[7] Professor Stengel suggests that, 'it is reasonable not to accept the suicidal act alone as a criterion of one of the typical mental disorders.'[68] He states that 'on the average one third of the people who commit suicide have been suffering from a neurosis or psychosis or a severe personality disorder.' Suicide is rare, he claims, among the mentally subnormal.

In these statements four categories of mental abnormality have been mentioned. Bearing in mind the complexity of the area we are considering and the fact that the dictionary definitions of the terms used by Professor Stengel in the statement quoted do not afford an adequate explanation, it may be worth giving a brief indication of what is meant. The first of the categories referred to was *neurosis* and this, to borrow the definition offered by Dr Eric Berne,[16] is 'characterised by excessive use of energy for unproductive purposes' to the detriment of personality development. Examples include *hypochondriasis*, in which the individual uses his energy to 'love himself', continually observing the reactions of his body and taking alarm at the slightest irregularity, and *phobias* such as spermophobia, in which the fear of germs induces extravagantly rigorous and frequent washing of the hands. The second of the categories mentioned, *psychosis*, is a serious disturbance in which there is a break with reality. 'Psychosis', says Dr Berne, 'is the medical word roughly corresponding to the legal term insanity.' Examples include *schizophrenia*, in which the sufferer's behaviour is a response to what is going on in his head regardless of the realities around him, as in the obedience to the commands of imaginary voices, and *paranoia*, in which the victim is convinced that the behaviour of those around him is intended to harm him. The third category mentioned in the quotation from Professor Stengel was severe *personality disorder*. This includes hysteria, in which the sufferer reacts to frustration with symptoms such as paralysis or amnesia; it also includes alcoholism. The last of the four categories, *mental subnormality*, refers to those whose mental development has been retarded, including the severely handicapped.

It is not within the scope of this book to explore the causes, symptoms or treatment of mental abnormality. This is the realm of the psychiatrist and is the subject of a wealth of technical literature. There is one condition, however, which plays a significant role in the development of proneness to suicide and to which we must give some attention: this is depression, which when it is severe may be called *melancholia*. Once again we are confronted with a problem of definition. The word *depression* has a wide range of meaning. It is common to hear someone say he is depressed when what he means is that he is feeling a little down in the dumps. But *depression* may also be used to describe an illness that can lead to suicide. The fact that the same word is used for the two extremes may indicate that there is a qualitative similarity between the ephemeral feelings known as the *the blues* and the chronic despair of melancholia, but it may conceal a deadly disparity. There is, it seems, a wide spectrum of symptoms that are covered by the term *depression* and this is reflected in the definition given by the U.S. National Association for Mental Health: 'Depression is an emotional state of dejection and sadness, ranging from mild discouragement and downheartedness to feelings of utter hopelessness and despair.'[69]

The onset of depression may be quite sudden, even dramatic, or it may be insidious. The condition is characterized by feelings of utter hopelessness, a sense that at best the present is an empty charade and that the future can offer nothing better. Life is felt to be pointless. 'Dead Faith, dead Love, dead Hope', says James Thomson.[29] Weariness seems invincible.

> Do not wonder that my body sinks to decay;
> Though my limbs are old, my heart is older yet,[70]

says the Chinese poet. Life may even be felt to be torment. All thoughts are turned inwards and any comparison that is made with the circumstances of those around the victim only serves to deepen his melancholy:

> I never knew another man on earth
>   But had some joy and solace in his life,
>   Some chance of triumph in the dreadful strife:
> My doom has been unmitigated dearth.[29]

It may be that here there is at least a partial explanation of the seasonal variation in suicide rate referred to in Chapter 1 (Appendix, Diagram 2). It has been suggested that this variation may in some way be 'the manifestation of one of the rhythmical biological changes which play an important part in animal life although they are much less conspicuous in man.'[68] For Durkheim, however, the key factor determining the springtime rise in the suicide rate is a social one: this is the time when there is a general resumption in activity after the stagnation of winter. Alvarez puts it nicely: 'the impulse to take one's life increases in the spring not because of any mysterious biological changes but because of the lack of them. Instead of change, there is stasis.'[71] Then he goes on:

> A suicidal depression is a kind of spiritual winter, frozen, sterile, unmoving. The richer, softer and more delectable nature becomes, the deeper that internal winter seems, and the wider and more intolerable the abyss which separates the inner world from the outer. Thus suicide becomes a natural reaction to an unnatural condition. Perhaps this is why, for the depressed, Christmas is so hard to bear. In theory it is an oasis of warmth and light in an unforgiving season, like a lighted window in a storm. For those who have to stay outside, it accentuates, like spring, the disjunction between public warmth and festivity, and cold, private despair.*

In other words, the activity of spring represents for most of us an increasing involvement in life, but for the depressed and suicidal it merely serves to exacerbate their sense of isolation. The external renewal contrasts cruelly with the private feeling of hopelessness.

The comparisons the depressed person makes between himself and those around him are usually negative and may produce in him feelings of worthlessness. These can extend into self-hatred and a desire for self-punishment. The victim may believe that his suffering is in some way justified, and the consequence of his failure or sin. His state of mind is an extremely unhappy and distressing one. And yet, as Freud has said,

> the self-torments of melancholiacs, which are without doubt pleasurable, signify a gratification of sadistic tendencies and of hate, both of which relate to an object and in this way have been turned round upon the self. In the end the sufferers usually succeed in taking revenge, by the circuitous path of self-punishment, on the original object who occasioned the injury and who is usually to

---

* T. S. Eliot (*The Waste Land*, Faber and Faber 1975) expressed it thus:

> April is the cruellest month, breeding
> Lilacs out of the dead land, mixing
> Memory and desire, stirring
> Dull roots with spring rain.
> Winter kept us warm, covering
> Earth in forgetful snow, feeding
> A little life with dried tubers.

be found in their near neighbourhood. No neurotic harbours thoughts of suicide which are not murderous impulses against others redirected upon himself.[72]

A high proportion, possibly 75 per cent, of those who fall victim to severe depression harbour thoughts of suicide and some of them, probably more than 10 per cent, make actual attempts to kill themselves.

There are many forms of depression and, says Zilbergeld, little agreement on what they are and what to call them.[73] It is convenient to distinguish between depressions which arise in the course of, and possibly as a consequence of, other illnesses, and those which are not associated with other disorders. The latter are termed *primary*, while the former are said to be *secondary*. Another way of categorizing depressions is in terms of polarity, *bipolar* depressions being those in which the sufferers' periods of despair alternate with spells of euphoria, and *unipolar* depressions, in which any relief from the despair is a return only to a normal mood. Perhaps the most frequently encountered classification of depressions is that which recognizes two main groups: *reactive* depression and *endogenous* depression. As the word suggests, *endogenous* depression appears to originate from within the sufferer and to have no external trigger. *Reactive* depressions, which are more common and usually less severe than the endogenous type, arise as a result of some occurrence or circumstance in the victim's life.

A number of questionnaires have been devised to permit assessment of depressiveness. They explore a range of aspects of the patient's life such as feelings of sadness, guilt, irritation and anxiety, and loss of weight, appetite and the ability to sleep. None of them, however, is infallible and diagnosis by experienced professionals is the only safe guide. Nevertheless it is possible to outline some of the chief indications of depression. In reactive depression there is a depression of mood, which tends to be variable in intensity, becoming more severe in the evening and when the sufferer is alone. The victim tends to be anxious and irritable and has some difficulty in going to sleep and in achieving a normal period of unbroken sleep. The endogenous depressive tends to display continuous depression, which is usually worse in the morning. There is a slowing down of physical and mental activity. Sleep patterns are usually severely disturbed, with early morning wakening a common feature. There is usually a marked loss in energy, appetite, weight and sexual drive and frequently the victim is agitated. He has a sense of uselessness and inferiority and may suffer from feelings of guilt. This loss of self-esteem, which is common in endogenous depression, rarely arises in the depression resulting from external circumstances. It can develop to the point where the sufferer's frame of mind is irrational. He feels that he is totally worthless and that not only is he abandoned by friends and family but he deserves to be. This sense of the need for punishment may in those of a strongly religious persuasion lead to a belief that they are beyond salvation and face eternal damnation; in others it may strengthen the suicidal thoughts that have perhaps already occupied their minds. Often the victim of severe depression, though feeling suicidal, is unable to take the positive action that will lead to his death. For him the greatest period of risk is likely to be in the early stages of treatment, when there is a gradual return of the energy to act.

Not all depression is readily recognizable. The psychological symptoms referred to above are not always obvious. Instead the victim complains of purely physical symptoms for which no physiological cause can be identified. Those around him may quite understandably conclude that the aches and pains of which he speaks are purely imaginary and they may come to regard him as a hypochondriac. Only careful questioning by a medical practitioner is likely to reveal that depression is the underlying cause. The same may be true of a sudden dependence upon alcohol or hard drugs. Alcoholism can be a consequence of depression. It can also be the cause, and the growing dejection of the alcoholic can in the end lead to suicide. Some workers have considered alcoholism to be a form of self-destructive behaviour, believing that the alcoholic is in fact trying to drink himself to death. Be that as it may, we have in the depressive's resort to alcohol the makings of a vicious circle, and the ultimate outcome of addiction is frequently suicide. The statistics quoted at the beginning of this chapter speak for themselves. What is true for alcoholism is also true of addiction to hard drugs. Thomas De Quincey tells us in *The Confessions of an English Opium-Eater* how he started to take opium.[74] It was toothache that first drove him to the drug, but it was misery that made him a habitual opium user. He confesses that his gloom was caused by 'youthful distresses in London' due to his own 'unpardonable folly'. It was, he claims, no passing affliction that might have soon departed but rather a 'settled and abiding darkness', in the words of Milton,

O dark, dark, dark, amid the blaze of noon,
Irrecoverably dark, total eclipse
Without all hope of day![75]

Happily De Quincey did accomplish his escape from his addiction, but not before experiencing deep despair. Writing of the effect of opium on his dreams he goes on,

[The] changes in my dreams were accompanied by deep-seated anxiety and funereal melancholy, such as are wholly incommunicable by words, I seemed every night to descend — not metaphorically, but literally to descend — into chasms and sunless abysses, depths below depths, from which it seemed hopeless that I could ever re-ascend. Nor did I, by waking, feel that I *had* re-ascended. Why should I dwell upon this? For indeed the state of gloom which attended these gorgeous spectacles, amounting at last to utter darkness, as of some suicidal despondency, cannot be approached by words.[74]

What causes depression? There are many answers to this question. It seems likely that some people are genetically predisposed to depression, that is to say that though the *cause* may not be an inherited characteristic there may be an inborn susceptibility in certain individuals. It is possible also that there may be changes in brain chemistry associated with depressive states. The presence of chemicals known to induce certain mental conditions does not, however, demonstrate that the *cause* is chemical; nor does the success or partial success of treatment based on drugs which control the level of these chemicals. The mechanism by which depression is produced may be explicable in terms of brain chemistry, but we have yet to establish what stimulates the biochemical changes involved. It is known that depression can be produced by changes in environment or circumstances: isolation, stress and loss are all liable to lead to it. There is evidence, too, that some people become depressed as a result of food allergies. Certain infections are known to cause depression, as are some surgical operations. Childbirth is not infrequently succeeded by a period of post-natal depression. And like many other ailments depression is often associated with certain times in the menstrual cycle. Freud maintained that the roots of depression can be traced back to childhood, for example to the absence or loss of a parent.

There are many models of depression. Just as there are several schools of psychoanalysis so there have been several models advanced by the psychoanalysts, including that of Freud alluded to above. Not surprisingly, other, different models have been offered by the behavioural school of psychologists, emphasizing the learned nature of depressive behaviour, for example through the reinforcing effect of the normal sympathetic response to displays of depression. Other models suggest a biological basis for depression. None of these various models can be regarded as providing more than a provisional representation of what underlies depression, though each has some value in the development of treatments. The biological models lead to the formulation of antidepressant drugs and the success of these can often be dramatic. A patient seriously affected by depression can in a few weeks be brought to normality and those in contact with him can be surprised by the change in thinking from total negativity to the more positive outlook that prevailed before the onset of the depression. Similarly the use of ECT (electro-convulsive therapy), in which an electric current is applied to the skull under an anaesthetic, can be very effective. No one can be sure how ECT works, but in some cases the results are impressive: a single brief treatment can return the patient to normal health. John White, a Christian psychiatrist refers in his book, *The Masks of Melancholy*,[76] to the possibility of divine healing, the casting out of demons responsible for mental distress. Bernard Rosenblum, an American psychiatrist and a believer in astrology, suggests that

> clients who feel that astrology is philosophically more meaningful to them than psychotherapy, who fear the 'dredging-up' aspects of therapy and feel a real emotional contact with an astrologer could probably be helped more in the astrological situation than in the psychotherapeutic one.[77]

I mention this not from any personal conviction about the significance of astrology but to illustrate how it is possible to use a variety of models as the basis for successful treatment.

One of the major treatments for depression is psychotherapy. It takes the form of a series of conversations with a trained therapist. The purpose of these is to enable the patient to examine his own attitudes, behaviour, fears and hopes. Once again the method adopted depends upon the particular model the therapist uses. Behavioural therapy is one approach and it proceeds from the view that depressives get less pleasure from their activities than other people do from theirs. The therapist aims to reduce depressive responses, perhaps by ignoring them, and to reinforce more positive behaviour. Attempts are made to develop greater assertiveness and to focus on rewarding experiences. Cognitive therapy on the other hand starts from the premise that the patient's problems stem from the way he misinterprets events; in other words the cause of the problem is wrong thinking. Dorothy Rowe, in her award-winning book, *Depression — The Way Out of Your Prison*,[78] describes how depressives are responsible for their own condition. 'Depression', she writes, 'is not a genetic fault or a mysterious illness which descends on us. It is something which we create for ourselves, and just as we create it so we can dismantle it.' She shows how wrong and negative attitudes are developed and preserved. 'There are many ways in which a person can work out the equation, being depressed = being good.' She describes how she uses a technique of 'laddering' to demonstrate to her patient how the most simple decision he takes is linked to the way he values his existence. By starting off with a simple question of choice, say, of two out of three kinds of food, and by a process of 'Why-is-it-important?' questions she leads her patient to an encounter with his deepest feelings about existence. It is a process, she suggests, that one can perform for oneself. The hardest change to make, she argues ('If you can manage this, the rest is easy'), is to treat oneself kindly. It is an ancient wisdom. As the fifth-century Buddhist commentator, Buddhaghosa, said, love for all includes love for oneself.[79]

Anthony Storr in his book, *The Integrity of the Personality*,[80] observes that the results of psychotherapy do not seem to depend upon the school to which the therapist belongs or on the methods he uses. 'In my search for an explanation of the efficacy of psychotherapy', he writes, 'I am forced to the conclusion that the underlying common factor is the development of the relationship between the patient and the psychotherapist.' He goes on to emphasize that the relationship should not be one in which the therapist relies predominantly on suggestion but rather one in which it is constantly demanded that the patient should solve his own problems. As Zilbergeld puts it,

> in some ways therapy is similar to prayer. Both can be comforting and useful even when one does not get what one asks for. Both can keep hope alive; combat boredom and demoralization; decrease loneliness and alienation; help us to get things off our chests and clear our minds; and make us feel more in control and more confident.[73]

There are, of course, skills which can be learned and some writers on depression have positive suggestions to make. Dr Caroline Shreeve in her book, *Depression, Its Causes and How to Overcome It*,[81] outlines a programme which she has found effective. It includes a cold bath every morning, daily practice of some kind of aerobic exercise, listening to music, the use of incense sticks, adoption of a wholefood diet and the practice of *looking and seeing* several times each day. She also advocates a regimen of relaxation exercises and a positive approach to matters which are causing stress, worry and anxiety.

She suggests that some people might find it beneficial to adopt the affirmation technique developed by Émile Coué for improving self-confidence; this entails repeating several times each day some positive statement such as 'Every day, in every way I'm getting better and better.' Others, Dr Shreeve believes, might find it useful to learn autohypnosis and she outlines a method. One difficulty, of course, is that the motivation of those who are depressed is often so low that they are unlikely to embark upon a programme of self-help; in such cases hospital treatment may be the only solution, but the kind of approach Dr Shreeve describes may be very relevant to those who are capable of responding to it.

In his book, *Overcoming Depression*,[69] Dr Andrew Stanway discusses the various symptoms of depression and offers some advice to family and friends on the most helpful responses they can offer. Like the advice of Dr Shreeve, what Dr Stanway suggests is of a practical nature and could be of considerable comfort to those who are faced with the difficult and demanding problem of living with a depressive. He summarizes as follows:

> The 'cure' for depression, of both its symptoms and its causes, must lie in more love. A feeling of being loved and wanting to love in return can make up for all those feelings of emptiness and low self-esteem that so dog the depressed. We're all lovable in some way to some people. Love is the great protector or, as Freud so aptly put it, 'In the final analysis, we must love in order not to fall ill.'

Research into means of dealing with depression goes on. In *The Sunday Times* of 14 April 1985 there was a report that for certain forms of depression exposure to bright light is a possible cure. Some people, it is claimed, reveal a seasonal pattern of depression in the autumn and winter alternating with improved or even manic states in the spring and summer. The success of trials carried out in America by Dr Norman Rosenthal of the US National Institute of Mental Health encouraged Dr Stuart Checkley to evaluate the treatment at the Maudsley Hospital in London. Another equally surprising approach was the subject of an item in *The Listener* for the 25th of the same month, which dealt with smiling. It pointed out that Darwin had described facial expressions as a form of communication. Thus animals bare their teeth to signal aggression to other animals. Human beings have developed a wide range of facial expressions, including those which indicate fear. The question arises: if, as Darwin suggests, all behaviour patterns have a survival value, what could be the advantage of being able to signal fear? Consideration of this has led Professor Zajonc of the University of Michigan to expand on the theory advanced in 1907 in a book, *Human Physiognomy, Its Mechanism and Social Role*, by a French doctor called Israel Waynbaum. Waynbaum suggested that since the brain and face receive their blood supply from the same artery, the carotid, the face serves as a reservoir or buffer vessel to keep the amount of blood in the brain steady. Zajonc rejects this explanation but suggests that the movement of facial muscles causes small changes in the flow of blood to certain areas of the brain, thus altering their temperature and thereby triggering the release or suppression of chemicals that affect the way we feel. Zajonc suggests that people who smile feel happy because they are stimulating the flow of chemicals which induce their feeling of well-being, and conversely those who wear a bleak expression are thereby making themselves *feel* bleak. Zajonc postulates that it might be possible to treat some depressions by means of some system of biofeedback which encourages the patient to smile.

There may be no truth in either of the theories just described. Certainly one would have to see a good deal of corroborative evidence before one could happily accept either. What they do, however, is to remind us of just how complex the human organism is and how little we know about how it operates. There is, of course, a danger that we confuse mechanism with cause, model with truth. Zilbergeld[73] quotes from Jeremy Leven's novel, *Satan*, in which the Devil complains,

> psychotherapy worries the hell out of me . . . It keeps turning evil into neuroses and explaining away people's behaviour with drives and complexes . . . Modern psychiatry is putting me out of business.

So, I shall conclude this brief look at depression by returning to the point made earlier, namely that there are many possible models and many possible treatments. It may be no more or no less true, no more or no less helpful, to say that depression is a metabolic disturbance than to think of it in the terms used by the psychiatrist David Burns in his book, *Feeling Good*:

> Depression is *not* a precious, genuine, or important human experience. It is a phony, synthetic counterfeit.

Both are true; neither is *the* truth. [82]

6.

BEREAVEMENT

> There are two parties to the suffering that death inflicts; and, in
> the apportionment of this suffering, the survivor takes the brunt.
>
> Arnold Toynbee, *Man's Concern With Death*

In his autobiography, *The Door Wherein I Went*,[83] Lord Hailsham
writes briefly and movingly of the suicide of his brother, Edward.
The plight of those bereaved by suicide could not be expressed
more clearly.

> Bereavement is one thing. The pain at bereavement is the price
> we pay for love, and high as that price is, it is not one which one
> grudges paying when bereavement is suffered. But bereavement
> by suicide is something altogether different and leaves an incurable
> wound. If only Edward had known the pain he was inflicting on
> us all who were left behind, and the ceaseless and incurable self-
> condemnation we all felt so that even now forty years later I cannot
> bear the burden of it, he would never have done what he did.

Lord Hailsham expresses the hope that by reading the account
of his experience other families might be spared from such
intolerable woe and in the vehemence of his denunciation of
suicide ('Suicide is wrong, wrong, wrong') he reveals how strong
his feelings are. It is little help to attempt to comprehend the state
of mind of the person who has taken his own life. We may know
that there could have been no intention to cause pain. We may
understand that the victim must have reached that stage of
constriction in which suicide seemed to be the *only* answer to
his despair. We may realize that even had we been permitted access
to his thoughts there would have been nothing that we could
have done to avert disaster. But our feelings of pain and guilt would
not be eased. Suicide is a negative and destructive act and the

feelings it leaves in those who are left are negative and destructive.

Bereavement is always an agonizing experience, but the grief which follows a natural or accidental death has a positive aspect. 'It's purpose,' says Tony Lake,

> is to enable us, over a period of time, to adapt to what has happened, and to bring us back to life. In the first shock of bereavement we are closer to death than to life. But through our grieving at the loss of those near to us, we can find ways eventually of living closer to life — closer, if our grieving can be complete, than perhaps we have ever lived.
>
> If you have ever asked yourself what is the purpose of life, then maybe you have recognized that most of us do not have a purpose, but many purposes. Grief renews all the purposes of our lives, whatever these might be. Grief allows us to feel and accept fear, anger and worry in new ways, and allows us also to experience greater joy and peace. Unlike death itself, grief is never wasteful nor pointless. [84]

The story is told of the Chinese philosopher, Chuang Tzu, that shortly after his wife died a friend visited him to offer condolences. Finding the philosopher sitting on the ground singing and beating time on an inverted bowl his friend expressed disapproval that he was not shedding tears. Chuang Tzu explains,

> When she died, I could not help being affected by her death. Soon, however, I remembered that she had already existed in a previous state before birth, without form, or even substance; that while in that unconditioned condition, substance was added to spirit; that this substance then assumed form; and that the next stage was birth. And now, by virtue of a further change, she is dead, passing from one phase to another like the sequence of spring, summer, autumn and winter. And while she is thus lying asleep in Eternity, for me to go about weeping and wailing would be to proclaim myself ignorant of these natural laws. Therefore I refrain. [85]

Anyone who has suffered bereavement will find Chuang Tzu's behaviour almost beyond belief, but the point of the story is sound. Death is 'a necessary end'. [86] 'He that begins to live, begins to die'. [87] Bereavement is a part of what it is to be a human being. 'The whole wide world weeps with thy woe', says the Buddha to the bereaved mother. [88]

But grieving, though it is natural and though its purpose and outcome may be positive, is all but unbearable. Its course is marked by a number of well-defined stages. It may begin before the death that causes it has actually taken place. There is sorrow in the reflection that those we love are mortal and the pain of bereavement can begin with the anticipation of death. Perhaps this arises when an illness is diagnosed as terminal. However clear the intimations of death, *full* realization eludes us and, though grief may already have been felt, the moment of decease is traumatic. This may be especially so if the death has been wholly unexpected, the result of an accident or a seizure, when shock will be added to all the other emotions that arise.

There is inevitably a feeling of loss, of emptiness. Someone who has played an important role in our life is no longer there. Life may become meaningless. Shakespeare puts the following bitter words into the mouth of Macbeth when news is brought of Lady Macbeth's death:

> She should have died hereafter;
> There would have been time for such a word.
> Tomorrow, and tomorrow, and tomorrow,
> Creeps in this petty pace from day to day,
> To the last syllable of recorded time;
> And all our yesterdays have lighted fools
> The way to dusty death. Out, out, brief candle!
> Life's but a walking shadow, a poor player
> That struts and frets his hour upon the stage,
> And then is heard no more; it is a tale
> Told by an idiot, full of sound and fury,
> Signifying nothing.

The newly bereaved find it difficult to grasp, to accept, what has happened. It is a kind of numbness, almost as if nature were applying its own anodyne to blunt the pain of loss. Then there is anger: 'Why me?' And here those who believe in a deity in control of our destiny may rail against Him. It is as though the bereaved person feels the need to lash out in revenge. Often alternating with this feeling of anger there is a stage of denial, denial that the dead one has gone for ever, denial that he will not turn up again. The bereaved person may actually proceed to look for the lost person, expecting him to arrive home at the customary time or taking steps to make contact with him through spiritualism. There may also at this point be feelings of guilt, feelings that can be expressed in terms of 'If only I had . . .'

Gradually these stages are replaced by acceptance. The anger subsides; the searching is abandoned. The bereaved person begins to let go the lost one. It is the beginning of a new life, of regrowth. The time taken may be long. Sometimes the bereaved person sticks at one of the stages. He may, for example, continue with the denial stage, waiting for the miracle that will bring the loved one back. It may be, too, that he suffers from depression and some of the physical symptoms it can produce. Medical help may be appropriate, though the alleviation of the grieving process by means of drugs is of no real benefit. Like all suffering, grief is something that has to be worked through by the individual himself. But it is worse if he has to do so in isolation; human contact does help. The strength of the emotions involved, however, can act as a barrier to contact with other people, who may fear the pain and embarrassment of sharing the feelings of the bereaved person.

If all goes well life will return to normal, but this is not to say that there will be no scars. The nineteenth-century poet, James Thomson, author of the long and sombre poem, *The City of Dreadful Night*,[29] was himself the victim of a sad bereavement through the early death of Matilda Weller, with whom he had fallen in love. His own life ended prematurely through excessive drinking. The poem for which he is chiefly remembered was published in 1874, eight years before his death, and excerpts are to be found in many anthologies of English verse. Wishing to read the entire work, I obtained a copy from a library. It had been printed in 1888 and had not been read for a long time. The covers were falling from it. In it I came across three lines which some earlier reader had carefully marked with a pencil:

> The inmost oratory of my soul,
> Wherein thou ever dwellest quick or dead,
> Is black with grief eternal for thy sake.

How accurately these poignant lines voice the feelings of many who have suffered bereavement. There are many for whom the loss of a spouse, though accepted, has meant the closure of a part of their lives. It is for them as if the grieving process has been what Emily Dickinson called

> The Sweeping up the Heart
> And putting Love away
> We shall not want to use again
> Until Eternity.[89]

Many people in the throes of grief after a bereavement have

had suicidal thoughts. Life, it seems, is no longer worth living. Some have the idea that by hastening their own death they will bring closer the time when they will be reunited with those they have lost. More often, however, the suicidal thoughts are a reflection of the intolerable nature of their feelings. The number who actually take their own lives is fortunately not high but a minority do make suicide attempts. There is no evidence to indicate that those bereaved by suicide are more prone to ending their own lives. A number of workers have lent support, however, to the conclusion that bereavement as a result of suicide is likely to be more devastating than that incurred by death from other causes. One feature of bereavement by suicide is the likelihood that the relationship between the deceased and the bereaved has been fraught with stress. Other stressful factors that have been identified are the involvement of the police and blame placed on the bereaved by neighbours and family. This latter seems to stem from the notion that those who take their own lives have been driven to do so. Consequently the support offered to bereaved spouses is less if death has resulted from suicide than it usually is when the death has been from some other cause.

Lord Hailsham referred to the incurable self-condemnation he and his family felt after his brother's suicide. Workers have noted that guilt is an intense and long-lasting emotion in those bereaved by suicide. There is often a feeling that somehow the bereaved person failed by not preventing the act. The suicide is often regarded by the surviving spouse as an indictment of his inability to make life tolerable for the victim. Such feelings of guilt may be particularly persistent because of the difficulty the sufferers have in discussing them. It has been noted on the other hand that the disturbance caused in those bereaved by suicide, though initially more severe than that resulting from normal bereavement, is sometimes less severe in the long term than that experienced by the normally bereaved. It has been suggested that this could in some instances be explained by the fact that some suicides, however much distress they may cause in the short term, are in the long run a blessing to the survivors.

In conclusion it should be noted that it is not only successful suicidal acts which cause severe distress; attempted suicide is also highly disturbing to those close to the person involved. Doubtless, some of these attempts have been planned with a view to causing such distress, but this is certainly not universally the case. Nor is it the case that all suicide attempts are intended to be successful; in fact, it appears that the term *suicide attempt* may often be inappropriate. We shall examine this question in the next chapter.

7.

PARASUICIDE

Most people who commit suicidal acts do not either want to die or to live; they want to do both at the same time, usually the one more, or much more, than the other.

Erwin Stengel, *Suicide and Attempted Suicide*

Reference was made in Chapter 1 to the introduction of the term *parasuicide* to describe non-fatal acts in which self-injury is deliberate or a substance is ingested in excess of any prescribed or generally recognized therapeutic dosage. The frequency of such acts far exceeds that of suicide. Even allowing for the uncertainty of the data for both, it can be stated beyond doubt that the number of parasuicides occurring each year in England and Wales is of a different order of magnitude from that of suicide. The number of suicides in 1984 was 4,304; the figure for hospital admissions resulting from deliberate self-poisoning is estimated to be in excess of 100,000, and the actual number of parasuicides may be double this figure. Overdosing is, in fact, one of the most common reasons for admission to hospital and accounts for much of the strain placed on the staff.

Views differ on the relationship between suicide and parasuicide. In an obvious sense they share a common idea, though the level of intent may be different. Some workers have suggested that the two are ultimately connected. The more widely held view, however, is that we are dealing with two essentially different phenomena. The statistics certainly suggest that this is so. It has been noted, for example, that whereas the suicide rate for England and Wales fell steadily throughout the 1960s and 70s the incidence of parasuicide increased during this period. One possible reason for the increase of non-fatal overdoses is that the lethality of the substances used has declined. However, there are other reasons for thinking that parasuicide is a separate phenomenon. As has already been indicated, suicide is more prevalent among men than women. Parasuicide on the other hand is to be found more frequently among women. Moreover, whereas suicide increases with age among both men and women (though it declines in women in the 65 + age group) the parasuicide rate follows a virtually opposite trend. In the 15-16 age group the majority of parasuicides are women and for them the rate . thereafter declines steadily with age. In men the pattern is similar except that the highest rate is not reached until around 25, dropping steadily beyond this age.

Perhaps the most convincing reason for regarding parasuicide as something distinct from suicide is what many parasuicides have to say about their own behaviour. There are, of course, reasons for regarding many of these subjective comments with a measure of scepticism and we shall return to this aspect later in the present chapter. But when the circumstances of the act seem to confirm the statements of the person involved one is inclined to accept what is said. Thus, there are a great many occurrences in which overdoses have been taken in situations where discovery is almost inevitable. (That word *almost* has a certain significance, to which we shall return.) It *could* be that the choice of time and location has been a matter of misjudgement and that the intention has been to die, but the pattern is too common for error to be the cause. It *could* be that embarrassment lies behind the 'admission' that the act has not been intended to be fatal, but it is often embarrassment that leads people to claim that death *was* the intended outcome. No, I think we have to accept that there are many instances where the overdose does not have a fatal intent. I recall asking a man if he was feeling suicidal. He said that he was not, despite occasional periods of feeling low. I asked him if he had ever been prone to suicidal thoughts in the past. 'Oh, yes,' he said. He had taken several overdoses and had made many cuts in his wrists; he showed me the faint scars. 'But it was all make-believe,' he added. I believed him, but I wonder if he would have been able to admit this even to himself at the time he was making these 'attempts'.*

Attention was drawn above to the fact that many overdoses are taken in circumstances where discovery is *almost* certain. In

---

* The story has been disguised: for this and other reasons it is unidentifiable.

such cases the balance between the wish to die and the desire to live may be even. The individual may perceive this as uncertainty or as a matter of little importance. 'I really didn't care whether I lived or not' is the way it might be expressed. Often there is a desire not to have to decide but rather to leave the outcome to fate. This is why the arrangements made often leave an area of doubt as to whether someone will reach the scene in time. To the outsider this looks like gambling with life. Perhaps it is. If one considers the tossing of a coin as a means of making a choice to be gambling, then one must accept that there is an element of the lottery in many parasuicidal acts. The unfortunate individuals concerned, however, probably would not agree. It would be for them more a matter of leaving the decision to an external agency. 'I can't decide; someone else will have to.' Edward de Bono in *de Bono's Thinking Course*[90] pointed out that when the alternatives were equally attractive the decision should be easy because whichever choice is made will be acceptable. But this, he suggested, was not so and he illustrated the argument by reference to the philosopher Buridan's ass, which when it was placed between two equally succulent bundles of hay starved to death because it could find no reason why it should proceed in the direction of one rather than the other. De Bono's point was that in decisions where there is sufficient information for a logical choice to be made we humans are superfluous; the decisions are largely made for us. In the end, he argued, the decisions we do have to make are all emotional. There certainly seems to be no logic in the thinking that leads to a parasuicidal act. The choice that is made emerges from a turmoil of conflicting emotions. Is there any surprise, therefore, that resort is often made to chance?

Thus we can see that there is a whole spectrum of intention, from that of the person who is determined to die, through to the individual who has *no* wish to die (though he may have doubts about his desire to live). The outcome of the act is no reliable guide to its intention. Just as there are failed suicide attempts so there are parasuicidal acts that go wrong, and the person who has no real wish to die loses his life. One reason for this is ignorance about the lethality of the substance ingested. For example, it appears that many people do not realize how dangerous in overdose are some drugs (notably paracetamol) which are safe when taken in the prescribed amounts. Another complicating factor is that many parasuicidal acts are preceded or accompanied by the consumption of large amounts of alcohol, the effects of which may have a bearing on the level of intent when the act is performed.

In their book, *Attempted Suicide*,[91] Hawton and Catalán described work in which the survivors of overdoses were asked to choose from a list of possible explanations those that had been responsible for their behaviour. About one-third of the patients who were questioned indicated that they had wanted to die, a similar proportion said they had not minded either way and the remaining third admitted that they had not wanted to die. More than half chose as one of their reasons that their situation had been so unbearable that they had had to do something but did not know what. The next most frequently chosen reason was to get relief from a terrible state of mind. The third was to escape for a while from an impossible situation. Three other reasons came fairly high in the list of choices: 'you seemed to lose control of yourself and have no idea why you behaved in that way', 'show how much you loved someone' and 'make people understand how desperate you were feeling'. The clinical details of the patients involved were given along with transcripts of their interviews to three psychiatrists for comment. They agreed with the patients who had said they had had no wish to die, but they were in much less agreement with those who had said they had wished to die. One reason for this was that some of the patients had acted in a way that had guaranteed survival. The psychiatrists, who were not offered the reason most often selected by the patients, gave as their first four choices: 'make people understand how desperate you were feeling', 'frighten or get your own back on someone/ make people sorry for the way they have treated you', 'try to influence some particular person or get them to change their mind' and 'get relief from a terrible state of mind'. Clearly the patients' choices leaned towards avoidance of suffering, while the psychiatrists seemed to detect manipulative intentions. It is most interesting that neither the patients nor the psychiatrists chose with any great frequency the reason, 'seek help from someone'. This seems to cast doubt on the cliché that a suicide attempt is a cry for help. Hawton and Catalán suggest that there is more than one reason for most overdoses. For example, an overdose may serve to blot out an intolerable distress and at the same time make other people pay attention. Once again it appears that motive is a very private affair and that we can only guess at the feelings that lead to parasuicidal acts. In their book Hawton and Catalán refer to unpublished material by Bancroft and Hawton in which reasons are suggested for some of the claims that overdoses have been taken with the intention to die. One reason is that the patient feels that by insisting that there was a real wish to die he enhances the effect of his action on those it was intended to influence. Another reason suggested is that the patient feels a need to justify his behaviour to himself. Of course it is clear also that the reason given may be influenced by the attitude displayed by the medical and psychiatric staff dealing with the patient. There is a natural tendency for more sympathy to be shown towards those who, it is believed, truly meant to end their lives than those who are thought to have had manipulative intentions.

This distinction must surely be exacerbated in those cases where overdosing has been a repeating pattern of behaviour. A significant proportion of overdose patients have further episodes, repeats very often coming within a few months of previous occurrences. Bancroft and Marsack[92] suggested that there were three types of repeaters. First there were the chronic repeaters, for whom overdosing was an habitual method of coping with a crisis. Secondly there were those who made several repeats over a stretch of several months, for example during a period of marital stress, after which there was a long time when no overdoses were taken. Thirdly there were the one-offs, who took an overdose during a severe crisis and possibly made occasional repeats over the years. Barnes[93] identified a positive connection between the number of suicide attempts and the chance of having been the recipient of psychiatric treatment. The relevance of psychiatric conditions will be returned to later in this chapter.

Reference was made above to the overdose as a method of *coping* with crisis and one is reminded once more of the question asked by Fedden and quoted in Chapter 2: why when faced by a crisis do people make such an extraordinary gesture rather than evolve some other means of coping? Perhaps it is simply that when one is in extreme circumstances one hunts around for the most extraordinary thing to do. If one wishes to demonstrate how very unhappy one is one can do nothing more dramatic than show that the circumstances affect one's very will to live. This would seem to suggest that parasuicides are premeditated and have an objective other than the relief of misery. Many parasuicides, however, are the result of impulsive action and this is just one reason why prevention is so difficult. Another is that the situations that lead people to such action are always with us. A study carried out in Connecticut by Paykel, Prusoff and Myers[94] revealed that those who made suicide attempts tended to have a greater number of what the authors described as *life events* in the six months preceding the attempts than had been experienced by other people who had made no such attempts but whose depressive symptoms were similar. The life events to which reference was made included serious rows, illness or having to appear in court for an offence. The occurrence of such events was most frequently in the month preceding the overdose. A similar study by Bancroft and his colleagues[95] came to the same kind of conclusions. The events which preceded the self-injuries or overdoses were characterized by the fact that they were not part of the normal routine and it was most likely that they would involve either a member of the family or a boyfriend or girlfriend. A quarrel within a week of the attempt, and often within a day or two before it, was one of the most frequently reported events. Bancroft also found that where a chronic problem was involved, i.e. a difficulty that had persisted for more than a week prior to the attempt, it was most often to do with marital relationships or with a boyfriend or girlfriend. Less frequently the chronic problem was sexual, or to do with children, work or financial matters, or it was an accident or operation, or it was a difficulty associated with alcohol. Roberts and Hawton[96] found that the rate of parasuicide was high among parents who abused or neglected their children and also among those parents who were considered to present a risk of doing so. Both Morgan and his co-workers[97] in Bristol and Holding and his colleagues[98] in Edinburgh noted a high rate of unemployment among the male patients who had made attempts. Another study, carried out in Edinburgh by Steve Platt,[99] demonstrated a significant relationship between unemployment and parasuicide. He found that throughout the period of his study, that is from 1968 to 1982, there were increases both in the number of parasuicides among men and the male unemployment rate. Because, however, the increase in unemployment was much faster than the growth in the number of parasuicides the incidence of parasuicide among the unemployed actually *fell* between 1968 and 1982. Nevertheless, the incidence of parasuicide among the unemployed was much higher than in the rest of the male population. Another point to emerge from this study was that there was a significantly higher parasuicide rate among those who had been unemployed for long periods than for those who had been out of work for less than six months. This suggests that long-term unemployment is more conducive to parasuicide than is job loss. These relationships do not, however, prove a causal connection between unemployment and parasuicide. More work would be needed to show, for example, that there is not a common cause (economic recession) or that those who are prone to parasuicide are not more likely to become unemployed. Moreover, the causal connection between unemployment and parasuicide is not borne out by the results of interviews of parasuicides admitted to hospital; unemployment was not seen by them as being relevant to their action.

A minor proportion of parasuicides (5-8 per cent) suffer from severe psychiatric disorders, including schizophrenia. Stengel[68] observed that 'schizophrenics sometimes commit suicide, especially in the early stages of the illness when they may experience a sinister feeling of impending catastrophe.' It is known that those parasuicides who suffer from such severe disorders are more likely to take their own lives in the long run than those who do not. The majority of psychiatric disorders in cases of parasuicide are relatively minor and transient. The symptoms most frequently encountered during the weeks prior to an attempt are feelings of nervous tension, a depressed mood, a sense of hopelessness, irritability, tension pains, worrying and poor concentration.

As has been mentioned earlier, the frequency of parasuicide is highest among young women, especially those in the 15-20 age group, and it has been noted that the rate among younger teenagers has for some time been on the increase. A paper[100] published in 1985, however, refers to indications that there has recently been some evidence of a welcome decline. In the study[101] of fifty adolescents, forty-five of them girls and all in the age range 13-18, it was found that the most common problem was a recent row. Three-quarters of the group to which the study referred had had difficulties in their relationships with their parents, most commonly an inability to discuss problems with them; this was especially the case with their fathers. More than half had had problems at school, and among those who had left school unemployment and difficulties concerning their jobs were common. A half had had problems associated with boyfriends or girlfriends.

It has been found that a majority of overdoses are impulsive, many of them having been contemplated for less than an hour beforehand. It has been suggested that the individuals have been prepared for their parasuicidal behaviour by their past experience. This could either have been knowledge of other suicide attempts or it could have stemmed from childhood thoughts about, or responses to, parents of the 'You'll-be-sorry-if-I-die' type. The level of serious intent to die appears to increase with the degree of premeditation.

The most common method employed by parasuicides is to take an overdose of drugs, but some individuals adopt more violent approaches, such as wrist-slashing. Some people do this quite frequently and one may well deduce that their continued survival owes much to their skill in controlling the amount of damage they do. The proportion of parasuicides suffering from some kind of psychiatric disturbance is higher among those who use such methods, particularly when there is a history of repeated attempts. Not uncommon is the case of the woman who suffers from acute premenstrual tension and who has regular episodes of self-inflicted injury.

Clearly, when there are identifiable psychiatric causes treatment is possible, and it is common for victims of self-inflicted harm to be subjected to psychological assessment before they leave hospital. Prevention is another matter, especially where there is no illness to which the self-destructive behaviour may be attributed. We shall return to this aspect in Chapters 10 and 11.

8.

ATTITUDES TO SUICIDE

In the end, the suicide is rejected because he is so completely rejecting.

A. Alvarez, *The Savage God*

Our sympathies are most readily aroused by those with whom we can identify. It is easy to share the sorrow of a bereaved parent, but hard to feel for the plight of the brutal murderer. So it is with the common attitude towards those who are suicidal. We can commiserate with them over the circumstances that have led to their despair but we find it difficult to empathize with them in their rejection of life, which we treasure, perhaps above all else. Thus we may find talk of suicide distasteful or even incredible. There is a common belief — and it is totally fallacious — that those who speak of suicide do not take their own lives. It is often thought that the hints given of 'ending it all' are mere over-dramatizing or manipulation. This is contrary to experience, but it nevertheless reflects the feeling that suicide is unnatural. The inability to understand the need to articulate suicidal thoughts may even lead to a hostile response. This was revealed to me in an unexpectedly vehement outburst from a woman in one of the caring professions: 'I have no time', she said, 'for those people who tell you they are thinking of suicide; they should either shut up or get on and do it.'

Some of the revulsion against suicide has been engendered by the religious establishment, not only in this country, but elsewhere, and it has found expression in the law. In England the law was changed in 1961. Prior to that date suicide was regarded as self-murder and hence in the same category as homicide. Attempted suicide was treated as a misdemeanour and there were a significant number of prosecutions, some of those found guilty serving prison sentences. The Suicide Act 1961 established that suicide was no longer a crime and attempted suicide was not to be regarded as a misdemeanour, though it made a criminal offence the aiding, abetting or counselling of suicide by another person. Similar legislation had already been enacted in several other European countries, and suicide had not been treated as a criminal offence in Scotland for many years. Most insurance companies treat suicide as a natural risk, but they protect themselves against anyone taking out a policy with the intention of committing suicide as soon as it becomes valid and so benefiting dependants. This is done by the inclusion of a clause which invalidates the policy if the holder takes his own life within two years of its initiation.

Looking back to a period long before the new legislation, we can get some idea of the strength of feeling that prevailed by considering the ways in which the bodies of whose who had committed suicide were dealt with. In mediaeval times the body of the suicide was not permitted to receive a Christian burial. Instead of being placed in consecrated ground it was buried at a crossroads, a stake having first been driven through the body. Thomas Hardy in his novel, *Tess of the D'Urbervilles*,[102] refers to 'that shabby corner of God's allotment where He lets the nettles grow, and where all unbaptized infants, notorious drunkards, suicides, and others of the conjecturally damned are laid'. It seems that there were fears that there might be evil spirits associated with suicide; indeed it was thought that the suicidal act was the consequence of diabolical influence. Such views have also been held in societies outside the Christian world. Suicide was regarded as evil by certain African tribes and they were afraid of the dire consequences that might follow upon physical contact with the remains of a victim.[68] Alvarez refers to the practice adopted at Metz, where the body of a suicide was allowed to float down the Moselle in a barrel, thus removing it from the places it might wish to haunt. He mentions, too, that in Danzig the corpse of a suicide was not permitted to leave by the door but was instead lowered from a window, the frame of which was then burnt.[71] Josephus, the Jewish historian and a vehement opponent of suicide, describing it as 'a craven act', tells us how 'those who destroy themselves must by our rules be exposed unburied till sundown' though soldiers killed in battle, 'even our enemies, are thought to be entitled to burial.'[103] Josephus draws attention to the fact that 'in other lands it is laid down that the right hands of those who die thus should be cut off, since they have made war on themselves, on the ground that as the body has been divorced from the soul, so the hand must be divorced from the body.'

Durkheim tells us that the Spartan, Aristodemus, was posthumously punished for seeking, and finding, death at the battle of Platea, in which the Greeks defeated the Persians.[6] (Aristodemus's action was intended to wipe out the disgrace he had incurred by his absence from the earlier battle of Thermopylae.) Suicide by a soldier has in fact often been seen to be an act of cowardice or a dereliction of duty. Napoleon issued the following order of the day:

> The grenadier Groblin has committed suicide, from a disappoint- ment in love. He was, in other respects, a worthy man. This is the second event of the kind that has happened in this corps within a month. The First Consul directs that it shall be notified in the order of the day of the guard, that a soldier ought to know how to overcome the grief and melancholy of his passions; that there is as much true courage in bearing mental affliction manfully as in remaining unmoved under the fire of a battery. To abandon oneself to grief without resisting, and to kill oneself in order to escape from it, is like abandoning the field of battle before being conquered.[104]

It is reported, however, that Napoleon himself was not above reproach in this matter. After the retreat from Moscow he is said always to have carried with him a preparation of opium and when Josephine died he used it. The dose, however, was not fatal and he was persuaded to take an antidote.

Now no longer a crime, suicide is also less widely thought of in terms of sin, though even when it was so regarded there were always some churchmen who would not condemn it. What remains is a stigma, a sense of shame. It is painful enough to speak about the natural death of friends or family, but when the death has been self-inflicted we become aware of a sense of discomfort, a desire for reticence, which has nothing to do with grief. In his novel, *Ulysses*, James Joyce presents the following conversation between two of his characters. They are in a carriage on the way to attend a funeral.

> — In the midst of life, Martin Cunningham said.
> But the worst of all, Mr Power said, is the man who takes his own life.

Martin Cunningham drew out his watch briskly, coughed and put it back.

— The greatest disgrace to have in the family, Mr Power added.

— Temporary insanity, of course, Martin Cunningham said decisively.

We must take a charitable view of it.[105]

The feeling of disgrace may not be quite as strong as it was in Ireland at the time of which Joyce was writing, but the embarrassment that Martin Cunningham attempts to cover up with his cough and his hasty look at his watch are still to be found.

How charitably we look on suicide seems to depend upon the circumstances that have led to it. Our condemnation is more likely to be withheld if we accept that the circumstances were intolerable or if there is evidence of mental disturbance. Sometimes a suicide can generate considerable anger in those affected by it. In a courageous and outspoken letter published in *The Literary Review*[106] Germaine Greer expressed some of the anger she felt at the suicide of Julian Jebb. An important figure in London literary circles, Jebb had suffered from a drink problem. Germaine Greer's letter was written as an open one to the dead man. In it she says:

We've been summoned to a wake, but I'm not going. I haven't the stomach for it. I've seen too much of suicide; it oppresses me. I think after all that the right we have to kill ourselves is a legalistic notion. We've cost the world too much; we owe it at least a life.

She goes on to comment on his background. Then she continues:

You were capable of pleasures that other people have never been able to dream of because you were educated as a receptor of a special kind. Your penalty was anguish and anxiety of an equally special kind, but if you cared for the tradition you were bred to serve you would have borne them.

Perhaps you think the rest of us have an easier time than you did. Do you think we care less about cruelty, stupidity, insensitivity, inept editing, deliberate misconstruction, doltish incomprehension, the insolence of officialdom, the spurns that patient merit of the unworthy takes, than you did? By removing yourself you make the struggle harder for the rest of us. I think you know that, and I think by your last action you show us that you don't care. That's what hurts, the thought that finally dissolves the hard knot of anger and brings the relief of mourning.

You weren't friendless; you weren't ill; you weren't loveless; you weren't unemployed; you weren't broke; but you wanted to be dead. It's odd, isn't it? I've seen people in agony and dreadful insecurity struggling to survive war and plague and massacre, and have come home to see the lords of creation chucking their lives away.

There is anger there but there is also sorrow. Indeed, our reactions to suicide are complex. We can be saddened, angered, embarrassed, condemning and even nauseated. Flaubert tells us that when he was writing about Emma Bovary's death he twice vomited his dinner.[107] When we contemplate the act itself, the mechanics of death, we have very different feelings than when we recall the person or the circumstances and the despair of his last days. 'However beautiful the rest of the play,' wrote Pascal, 'the last act is bloody.'[108] Speaking to those bereaved by suicide I have found that often the one part of the story they find hard to tell is the act itself. It is at this point that we find it most difficult to form a picture in our minds. Can we possibly visualize the placing of the rope, the plastic bag, the leap, Emma Bovary 'cramming' the poison into her mouth?

And yet, we are prepared to watch drama in which suicide is the climax. We find the experience cathartic. Shakespeare, as we have already observed made much use of suicide in his plays. A glance through *Kobbé's Complete Opera Book*[109] reveals some forty operas in which suicide is represented. Some of these are among the most popular in the repertoire: Puccini's *Tosca* and *Madame Butterfly*, Verdi's *Aida*, *Ernani*, *Otello* and *Rigoletto* (Gilda), Wagner's *Die Walküre* (Brünnhilde), Bellini's *Norma*, Britten's *Peter Grimes* and many more. We read about suicides in some of the greatest literature ever written. But we speak warily of it.

The attitude towards suicide varies in the different strata of society. Richard Hoggart in his excellent study of working-class culture, *The Uses of Literacy*,[110] indicates that in the social environment of which he writes there is little opportunity for the hushing up of suicides we might find in other social milieux.

I remember too that in our neighbourhood we accepted suicides as a moderately common occurrence. Every so often one heard that So-and-so had 'done 'erself in', or 'done away with 'imself', or 'put 'er 'ead in the gas-oven', since the gas-oven was the most convenient means of self-destruction. I do not know whether suicide took place more often in the sort of groups I am speaking of than in middle-class groups. It did not happen monthly or even every season, and not all attempts succeeded; but it happened sufficiently often to be part of the pattern of life. Among the working-classes it could not be concealed, of course, any more than a row could; everyone quickly knew about it. The fact I want to stress is that suicide was not felt to be simply a personal matter or one confined to the family concerned, but was felt to be bound up with the conditions of the common life. Sometimes the cause was that a girl had 'got 'erself into trouble' and for one reason or another could not go through with it; just as often it was that, for those who put their heads on a pillow inside the oven-door, life had become unendurable; they were ill and treatment seemed to be doing no good; they were out of work; or, whatever they did, the debts piled up. This was not long ago. The fact that suicide could be accepted — pitifully but with little suggestion of blame — as a part of the order of existence shows how hard and elemental that life could be.

Attitudes to suicide differ, of course, from country to country. To give one example, suicide plays a part in Japanese culture quite unlike that occupied in ours. Whilst we have always admired selfless courage we have had nothing to compare with the Japanese Kamikaze pilots. These young men were willing to kill themselves for their country. The enthusiasm with which they adopted their role is revealed in the following extract from the diary of one of them:

> I am actually a member at last of the Kamikaze Special Attack Corps. My life will be rounded out in the next thirty days. My chance will come! Death and I are waiting. The training and practice have been rigorous, but it is worth while if we can die beautifully and for a cause. [111]

The Japanese practice of Hara-kiri is repugnant to us and no more so than in the recent, horrendous death of Yukio Mishima. 'He committed suicide to complete his literary work' was how one Japanese literary critic put it. [112] It would be of only limited value to give an account of Mishima's death, since it would not be representative of suicides encountered elsewhere. Those who are interested are referred to the excellent and readable biography, *The Life and Death of Yukio Mishima*, [112] written by Henry Scott Stokes. Let it suffice to say that Mishima was obsessed with the notion of a 'beautiful death' and in his view the beauty lay in the agonizing nature of the method he chose, ritual disembowelment. His was an extreme attitude not typical of his countrymen and it owed much to his sexuality, narcissism and exhibitionist tendencies. Nevertheless it was an extension of a strand of the Japanese experience with its roots in Samurai culture.

The Kamikaze mentality is not confined to Japan. Although their religions are, as we shall see in the next chapter, against suicide, adherents of Islam and Buddhism have in recent times displayed a willingness to become martyrs for their causes. Young Shi'ite extremists have blown themselves up to destroy their enemies. Buddhist priests have immolated themselves in Vietnam. We find such practices repugnant. This is possibly because we are not deeply involved with the conflicts of which they are a part. No doubt those who share the views of the martyrs find their self-destructive acts highly praiseworthy. Our own history has been well endowed with selfless acts of heroism and we speak with pride of those who 'gave their lives for their country'. Arguably many of those whose courage led them to death could not be described as suicides. One example, however, will illustrate our own attitude. We may no longer regard Captain Scott's ill-fated expedition to Antarctica with the same enthusiasm that was felt by his contemporaries. We may feel that it was badly planned and foolhardy. But surely none of us can remain unmoved by the story of Captain Oates, who walked out into a blizzard rather than be a burden to his comrades.

There have always been those who regarded suicide as an acceptable way of coping with misfortune. Zeno, who founded the philosophy of the Stoics, held that one was at liberty to abandon life if one found it not worth living. At the age of 98 he practised what he had preached: as he was leaving the school of philosophy one day he fell and put a toe out of joint; thereupon he went home and hanged himself. Seneca, another Stoic, made his position clear in the following words:

> I will not relinquish old age if it leave my better part intact. But if it begins to shake my mind, if it destroys its faculties one by one, if it leaves me not life but breath, I will depart from the putrid or tottering edifice. I will not escape by death from disease so long as it may be healed, and leaves my mind unimpaired. I will not raise my hand against myself on account of pain, for so to die is to be conquered. But if I know that I must suffer without hope of relief, I will depart, not through fear of pain itself, but because it prevents all for which I would live.[113]

The idea of suicide as a means of escape has been held by many. Seneca himself said, 'Against all the injuries of life, I have the refuge of death.' Epictetus, another Stoic, made the same point:

Remember that the door is open. Do not be a greater coward than the children, but do as they do. Children, when things do not please them, say, 'I will not play any more'; so when things seem to you to reach that point, just say, 'I will not play any more' and so depart, instead of staying to make moan.[114]

Cyril Connolly, writing as Palinurus in *The Unquiet Grave*, put it thus: 'When even despair ceases to serve any creative purpose, then surely we are justified in suicide.'[115] And Nietzsche summed it up in these words: 'The thought of suicide is a great consolation: by means of it one gets successfully through many a bad night.'[116]

The thought of suicide as a consolation lies behind the acceptance by many of the ideas held in our own day by the Voluntary Euthanasia Society. Death is our destiny and of itself is no more frightening than was the state we were in before birth, many of its members would say. What *can* be distressing is the process of dying or of physical and mental disintegration. People should, the proponents of voluntary euthanasia would argue, have the right to choose the time and manner of their depature. The surgeon, Dr Christiaan Barnard, puts the case for euthanasia in his book, *Good Life Good Death*.[117] In it he tells the story of a 78-year-old man admitted to hospital and given continued treatment in spite of his repeated requests to be allowed to die with dignity. 'The engine is broken down,' he said, 'it is time for the engineer to abandon it.' One night he reached out of his bed and switched off his life-support system and died. A note he left for his surgeon read: 'Death is not the enemy, Doctor. Inhumanity is.'

Dr Barnard refers to a film which depicted a suicide parlour where one could have an easy death administered in pleasant circumstances. 'I cannot think of a more civilized approach to the problem,' he writes. 'Suicide is a basic human right and should be an option always available to the individual.' Not everyone will agree with such a view. There will be many who are unable to approach the subject with the surgeon's dispassion. But the idea of euthanasia is certainly being discussed more openly and with less strength of reaction nowadays than one might have expected a few years ago. Dr Barnard is well aware, however, that his arguments will meet opposition:

For centuries, men have been disquieted by the occurrence of suicide in their midst. Most men have found it not only incomprehensible but also contemptible that some of their fellows should show a wilful preference for death, thus disdaining the existence to which others cling with such tenacity. Such persons, it is said, are unbalanced, mentally incapable of appreciating their good fortune in being alive.[117]

He is right. It has always been so. For every Seneca or Epictetus, for every John Donne defending suicide in his *Biathanatos*, for every Christiaan Barnard advocating suicide parlours and euthanasia, there has always been a multitude in opposition. Each time someone takes his own life there is a Germaine Greer thinking, if not passionately declaring, that he shouldn't have done it. When we are in a life-loving, creative frame of mind we feel he must have been unhinged. When we are finding life a trial we may feel angry with him. 'Any man who, of his own will, tries to escape the treadmill to which the rest of us feel chained incites our envy, and therefore our fury.'[118] It is not surprising, therefore, that suicide has been a near-taboo topic. The very word has, for some of us, an ugly sound. Counsellors often find it easier to ask someone whether the thought of not waking up has ever seemed attractive than to say bluntly, 'Are you suicidal?' Even those who advocate voluntary euthanasia prefer to use the phrase, 'self-deliverance'. Sir John Betjeman's lines,

> Oh why do people waste their breath
> Inventing dainty names for death?[119]

are an apposite comment on the employment of such euphemisms.

There have been very few, if any, good jokes about suicide. Not surprisingly, it is not regarded by many as a source of mirth. Perhaps just because it *is* a taboo subject some humorists have been attracted to it. Cartoons often depict someone standing on a ledge high above the street, ready to jump, but the caption is usually about the situation that has placed him there. It is not the idea of suicide which makes us laugh; it is the fact that some trivial matter is being used as a pretext for it. It is not a new joke. When we see such a cartoon in *Punch* or *The New Yorker* it should come as no surprise if we have a sense of déjà vu. In the second century BC Lucilius said that after spending some money in his sleep, Herman the miser was so hopping mad that he hanged himself. Even Dorothy Parker's well-known rhyme is funny because it is a commentary on living rather than on dying:

> Razors pain you;
> Rivers are damp;
> Acids stain you;

And drugs cause cramp.
Guns aren't lawful;
Nooses give;
Gas smells awful;
You might as well live.[120]

H. L. Mencken's observation that suicide is belated acquiescence
in the opinion of one's wife's relatives is, likewise, funny because
it is a new version of the old mother-in-law story. A recently
published book of cartoons, *I Wasn't Kidding*,[121] is subtitled *How
to Commit Suicide so They'll NEVER Forget*. Its ability to make
fun of the suicide act perhaps tells us something about the way
our attitudes to entertainment have changed in recent years:
twenty years ago it might have been regarded as offensive; now
it is — yes — funny. So, too, I think, is Richard Eberhart's little
piece about suicide:

Then the eighty-year-old lady with a sparkle,
A Cambridge lady, hearing of the latest
Suicide, said to her friend, turning off
TV for tea, 'Well, my dear, doesn't it seem
A little like going where you haven't been invited.'[122]

Perhaps this says more about elderly ladies in Cambridge than
it does about suicide, but it provides a convenient point from
which to move to the question of the ethics of suicide.

9.

IS SUICIDE RIGHT OR WRONG?

Whose life is it anyway?

Brian Clark

In the consideration of the morality of suicide there are four options. We may decide that it is the inalienable right of the individual to dispose of his own life as he pleases; if he chooses to die by his own hand he is wholly justified in doing so. Alternatively we may adopt the diametrically opposed position that, no matter what the circumstances, suicide is invariably wrong. Or we may feel that the circumstances are paramount in determining our stance: some suicides may be justified; others are not. Finally, we may judge that right and wrong are inappropriate categories for suicide or indeed for any act: suicide is neither moral nor immoral; it is amoral.

Which of these options we select will depend at least in part upon our fundamental view of the nature of man. Do we think of ourselves as the creation of a supreme being or are we the result of the random action of natural forces in an accidental universe? Or perhaps we feel that man is an expression of the universe's urge towards self-awareness. Have we been put into the universe or have we emerged from it? Do we have free will or are all our acts determined by nature or controlled by some god? Perhaps freedom eludes us in most of our lives and is encountered only in higher states of consciousness or is demonstrated only in those actions that are not conditioned by our needs and desires. Do our lives have meaning, a given, inherent meaning, or are they wholly meaningless? Or do we have to discover or create our own meaning? Does the word 'ought' enter our lives; is there any reason why we *should* adopt one course of action rather than another? Is morality a purely subjective affair, or is there an absolute framework of right and wrong, of good and evil? These are questions that the individual must answer for himself. Or he may choose to live, feel forced to live, as an agnostic, facing but never resolving a sea of uncertainties. By withholding all indications of preference for any one of these options I may be seen to be adopting the view that not one of them is any better than the others. That is not so, but I believe that there is for each individual only that philosophy which, being true *for him*, enables him to cope with life, to get through his quota of suffering, to withstand the slings and arrows of outrageous fortune. There are, however, many who are obliged to live as Levin does, not knowing and not seeing the chance of knowing what they are and for what purpose they have been placed in the world.

Some of the great religions of the world have been unequivocal in their condemnation of suicide. Islam is one of these. The Koran declares that 'no one can die except by Allah's leave' and that when people's time for punishment arrives 'they cannot tarry a single hour nor can they go ahead'.[123] For those who attempt to disobey the commands of Allah there is the ever-present threat of burning in the fires of Hell. Buddhism is also quite clear on the subject. Writing of the rules laid down for monks, Edward J. Thomas says in his *History of Buddhist Thought* that 'Suicide is condemned without qualification. On Buddhistic and general Indian theory it could only result in another life still burdened with the consequences of the individual's karma'.[79] How then do we explain the immolations of Buddhist priests in Vietnam, referred to in the previous chapter? On the one hand there is the evidence of the Buddha's first sermon, given to his disciples gathered in the Deer Park near Benares. He said that his followers should avoid devotion to the two extremes of the pleasures of the senses and of self-mortification, which he described as 'painful, unworthy [and] unprofitable.'[124] Burning oneself would surely be included in self-mortification. On the other hand there is a scripture (The Lotus of the True Law) which includes the suggestion that burning a finger or toe or some other member of the body in front of a monument of the Buddha is meritorious. This seems to have been an extension of the widely-held view that lighting a lamp in front of a statue of the Buddha is praiseworthy. Although there is no evidence that such self-cremation was ever practised in India, it appears that when the relevant scripture was translated into Chinese the idea was taken up and used in acts of religious devotion. It is probably in keeping with the old Chinese practice that the Vietnamese monks decided to sacrifice themselves rather than harm their persecutors. Thus although the immolations of the monks in Vietnam owed something to an ancient Chinese Mahayana Buddhist tradition they were contrary to the original teaching of the Buddha, known as The Middle Way.

It cannot be said that Hinduism has rigorously proscribed self-destruction. The practice of suttee is a case in point. In his prodigious book, *Philosophies of India*,[125] Heinrich Zimmer explains that the word suttee is derived from the Sanskrit *satī*, meaning 'a good and virtuous wife' and it was the name of the universal Goddess when she became incarnate to be the perfect wife of Śiva. Thus suttee, the immolation of a widow on her husband's funeral pyre, was 'an act consummating the perfect identification of the individual with her role, as a living image of the romantic Hindu ideal of the wife'. Gandhi, however, writing in 'A Reply to Rabindranath Tagore',[126] refers to the many letters he received begging him not to commit suicide as he had threatened. Some of them quoted verses from the great Hindu scripture, *The Bhagavadgītā*, showing that by taking his own life he would have been contradicting the teachings he held so dear. Gandhi does not say which verses were cited by his correspondents, but it is possible that the following might have been among them:

> To action alone hast thou a right and never at all to its fruits;
> let not the fruits of action be thy motive;
> neither let there be in thee any attachment to inaction.[127]

Gandhi's object in committing suicide would have been to put pressure on the British Government. Taken along with the Gītā's insistence on the merit of non-violence (which must surely include non-violence to self) the instruction, 'let not the fruits of action be thy motive', would seem to preclude his purposive self-destruction. For those whose suicidal thoughts are motivated by a desire to escape suffering the Gītā's counsel to be indifferent to the perception of pain and to show non-attachment to all desirable and undesirable happenings must have some relevance.

Judaic thought has emphasized the importance of preserving life, including one's own. Although suicide is not specifically forbidden in the Talmud, later authorities have deemed it a heinous sin, even worse than murder. There has, however, been a clear distinction between suicide and martyrdom, which under some circumstances has been regarded as highly meritorious. Four suicides are mentioned in the pre-Christian part of the Bible. One of these was Samson's; his self-inflicted death was a necessary consequence of his destruction of the Philistines in the house where they were offering sacrifice to their god, Dagon:

> And Samson said, Let me die with the Philistines. And he bowed himself with all his might; and the house fell upon the lords, and upon all the people that were therein. So the dead which he slew at his death were more than they which he slew in his life.[128]

This has, in Judaic thought, been considered as suicide *under mitigating circumstances*. The same has been thought of the deaths of Saul and his armour-bearer. Severely wounded by the arrows of the Philistines at Mount Gilboa, Saul wished to die.

> Then said Saul unto his armour-bearer, Draw thy sword and thrust me through therewith; lest these uncircumcised come and thrust me through and abuse me. But his armour-bearer would not; for he was sore afraid. Therefore Saul took a sword, and fell upon it. And when his armour-bearer saw that Saul was dead, he fell likewise upon his sword and died with him.[129]

The fourth instance was the death of Ahithophel, who, having asked that he should be allowed to pursue David and kill him, learned that Absalom had instead taken other advice.

> And when Ahithophel saw that his counsel was not followed, he saddled his ass, and arose, and gat him home to his house, to his city, and put his household in order, and hanged himself and died, and was buried in the sepulchre of his father.[130]

In his history of the war of the Jews against the Romans Josephus describes the mass suicide of the Jews at the besieged stronghold of Masada, a name which to this day is revered as an undying symbol of courage. Rather than submit to inevitable defeat, the Jewish garrison chose to die. The story is a ghastly one.

> '... let us deny the enemy their hoped-for pleasure at our expense, and without more ado leave them to be dumbfounded by our death and awed by our courage.' ... As if possessed they rushed off, everyone anxious to be quicker than the next man, and regarding it as proof positive of manliness and wisdom not to be found among the last: so irresistible a desire had seized them to slaughter their wives, their children, and themselves ... In the end not a man failed to carry out his terrible resolve, but one and

all disposed of their entire families, victims of cruel necessity who with their own hands murdered their wives and children and felt it to be the lightest of evils! Unable to endure any longer the horror of what they had done, and thinking they would be wronging the dead if they outlived them a moment longer, they quickly made one heap of all they possessed and set it on fire; and when ten of them had been chosen by lot to be the executioners of the rest, every man flung himself down beside his wife and children where they lay, put his arms around them, and exposed his throat to those who must perform the painful office. These unflinchingly slaughtered them all, then agreed on the same rule for each other, so that the one who drew the lot should kill the nine and last of all himself . . . [103]

(Josephus explains that, although these men died supposing that there were no survivors, two women and five small children escaped by hiding in the underground water conduits.) The conduct of the Jews at Masada is considered to be praiseworthy because they chose to die rather than surrender to the heathen. Another example is described in the book of Maccabees. It is a somewhat grisly tale of how Razis, one of the elders of Jerusalem, chose to die rather than fall prisoner to the Syrian General, Nicanor.[131] Present-day Judaic thought draws a distinction between suicide committed when the victim is of an unsound mind and that carried out by someone in full possession of his wits. Only the latter is considered reprehensible, and unless there is unmistakably clear evidence that the act has been voluntary and premeditated the verdict is usually suicide while of an unsound mind.

The early Christians seem to have disregarded suicide, but later it began to be thought of as a sin. St Augustine has a good deal to say on the subject in his book, *The City of God*. He adduces several arguments. First, he points out that it is contrary to the law for anyone to take it upon himself to kill a guilty person, and it is worse, he argues, to kill someone who is innocent. He abominates the suicide of the disciple, Judas. 'When he hanged himself he did not atone for the guilt of his detestable betrayal but rather increased it, since he despaired of God's mercy.' In ending his own life Judas was guilty not only of Christ's death but his own. Secondly, argued St Augustine, the suicide breaks the commandment, You shall not kill. Since, unlike the commandment against bearing false witness, there is no addition of 'your neighbour', this must include oneself. 'To kill oneself is to kill a human being.' Thirdly, he condemns suicide because it reveals a weakness of mind which cannot bear suffering. Fourthly, St Augustine deplores the notion that one might commit suicide to avoid possible sins in the future. Suicide, he says, is 'a detestable crime and damnable sin' and its commission is monstrous. 'Christians have no authority to commit suicide in any circumstance.' [132]

St Thomas Aquinas gave three arguments to prove that suicide was in conflict with natural law. First, he argued, suicide is contrary to the inclination implanted by the Creator in every creature to love itself and to preserve its own existence. Secondly, by taking his own life a man offends against society by depriving it of something rightfully belonging to it. And thirdly, suicide is an offence against God, who has given man his life to use and enjoy. [133] It is because of such arguments that the Roman Catholic Church holds suicide to be intrinsically evil. Graham Greene presents in his novel, *The Heart of the Matter*, [134] the dilemma faced by a Catholic who feels he has cause to commit suicide. Scobie, a police officer in an African colony, sends his wife away on holiday. While she is away he falls in love with Helen, a young widow. He concludes that it would be better for her if he were to die. He plans his suicide to look as if he has died from a heart attack. Afterwards his wife rejects the suggestion that his death might have been self-inflicted. 'Oh no, he wouldn't have done that,' she says. 'After all, in spite of everything, he *was* a Catholic.' A few hours before he dies Scobie, described by his wife as a bad Catholic, goes to church. Sitting there alone, he says:

> 'O God, I am the only guilty one because I've known the answers all the time. I've preferred to give you pain rather than give pain to Helen or my wife because I can't observe your suffering. I can only imagine it. But there are limits to what I can do to you — or them. I can't desert either of them while I'm alive, but I can die and remove myself from their blood stream. They are ill with me and I can't cure them. And you too, God — you are ill with me. I can't go on, month after month, insulting you. I can't face coming up to the altar at Christmas — your birthday feast — and taking your body and blood for the sake of a lie. I can't do that. You'll be better off if you lose me once and for all. I know what I'm doing. I'm not pleading for mercy. I am going to damn myself, whatever that means. I've longed for peace and I'm never going to know peace again. But you'll be at peace when I am out of your reach. It will be no use then sweeping the floor to find me or searching for me over the mountains. You'll be able to forget me, God, for eternity.'

Such sentiments may seem strange to the non-Catholic who does not share the kind of relationship with God that Scobie believes he has, but they indicate the horror of suicide that Catholics might feel. My own conversations with despairing Catholics have revealed that their religious beliefs are often a valuable obstacle to suicide. There have been few more eloquent expressions of Catholic revulsion against suicide than the following words of G. K. Chesterton:

> Not only is suicide a sin, it is the sin. It is the ultimate and absolute evil, the refusal to take the oath of loyalty to life. The man who kills a man, kills a man. The man who kills himself, kills all men; as far as he is concerned he wipes out the world. His act is worse (symbolically considered) than any rape or dynamite outrage. For it destroys all buildings: it insults all women. The thief is satisfied with diamonds; but the suicide is not: that is his crime. He cannot be bribed, even by the blazing stones of the Celestial City. The thief compliments the thing he steals, if not the owner of them. But the suicide insults everything on earth by not stealing it. He defiles every flower by refusing to live for its sake. There is not a tiny creature in the cosmos at whom his death is not a sneer. When a man hangs himself on a tree, the leaves might fall off in anger and the birds fly away in fury: for each has received a personal affront . . . There is a meaning in burying the suicide apart. The man's crime is different from other crimes — for it makes even crimes impossible.[135]

Such arguments could conceivably be levelled also at the martyr, but Chesterton thinks not:

> A martyr is a man who cares so much for something outside him, that he forgets his own personal life. A suicide is a man who cares so little for anything outside him, that he wants to see the last of everything. One wants something to begin: the other wants everything to end. In other words, the martyr is noble, exactly because (however he renounces the world or execrates all humanity) he confesses this ultimate link with life; he sets his heart outside himself: he dies that something may live. The suicide is ignoble because he has not this link with being: he is a mere destroyer; spiritually, he destroys the universe.[135]

What, one wonders, would Chesterton have made of Scobie?

It is not only from purely religious grounds that arguments have been advanced against suicide. St Thomas Aquinas's contention that self-destruction is contrary to the inclinations implanted by the Creator has been expressed in purely secular terms: it is unnatural. Spinoza in his *Ethics*[136] made the point thus:

> No one . . . unless he is overcome by external causes and those
> contrary to his nature, neglects to desire what is useful to himself
> and to preserve his being. No one, I say, from the necessity of his
> nature, but driven by external causes, turns away from taking food,
> or commits suicide, which can take place in many manners.
> Namely, any one can kill himself by compulsion of some other
> who twists back his right hand, in which he holds by chance his
> sword, and forces him to direct the sword against his own heart;
> or, like Seneca by the command of a tyrant, he may be forced
> to open his veins, that is, to avoid a greater evil by encountering
> a less; or again, latent external causes may so dispose his
> imagination and so affect his body, that it may assume a nature
> contrary to its former one, and of which an idea cannot be given
> in the mind. But that a man, from necessity of his nature, should
> endeavour to become non-existent, or change himself into another
> form, is as impossible as it is for anything to be made from nothing,
> as every one with a little reflection can easily see.

In response it might be said that calling something unnatural,
against nature, is a contradiction. T. H. Huxley defined nature
as 'nothing more or less than that which is; the sum of phenomena
presented to our experience; the totality of events past, present
and to come'.[137] This must encompass suicide. To say that a
particular pattern of behaviour is uncommon is one thing; to
suggest that therefore it is unnatural and consequently wrong
is quite another. Few of us would perform on the trapeze. To do
so would be uncommon and perhaps contrary to our instinct
of self-preservation, but would we call it unnatural or immoral?

Another of St Thomas Aquinas's arguments, that suicide is an
offence against society, has also been advanced outside the
Church. In the feudal system suicide was a breach of fealty. It
is recorded that in 1769 Blackstone wrote that 'the suicide is guilty
of a double offence: one spiritual, in invading the prerogative
of the Almighty . . .: the other temporal against the King.'[138]
Aristotle made the same point:

> . . . a man who cuts his throat in a fit of anger is voluntarily doing,
> contrary to the right principle, what the law does not allow;
> therefore he is acting unjustly. But towards whom? Surely not
> himself, but the state; because he suffers voluntarily, and nobody
> is voluntarily treated unjustly. It is for this reason that the state
> imposes a penalty, and a kind of dishonour is attached to a man
> who has taken his own life, on the ground that he is guilty of an
> offence against the state.[139]

(We might wish to ask whether the state is there for man's benefit or man for the state's.) The modern way of expressing this argument would be to assert that suicide is antisocial. The sociologist might attempt to refute this by suggesting that suicide is society's way of ridding itself of misery. The Utilitarian philosopher could conceivably condone suicide because it meets his criterion for what is right. The true measure of right conduct, he would say, is its consequences; so suicide would be considered justifiable if it removes pain or increases the sum total of human happiness.

Another argument advanced by Aristotle is reminiscent of Napoleon's order of the day, quoted in the last chapter:

> . . . to kill oneself to escape from poverty or love or anything else that is distressing is not courageous but rather the act of a coward, because it shows weakness of character to run away from hardships, and the suicide endures death not because it is a fine thing to do but in order to escape from suffering.[139]

Many have made the same point. Gustave Flaubert defined suicide as proof of cowardice.[140] One of Martial's *Epigrams* reads: 'The coward sneaks to death, the brave live on.'[141] Sir Thomas Browne put it more positively: 'When life is more terrible than death,' he said, 'it is truest valour to live.'[142] But Charles Caleb Colton reminded us in his *Lacon* that 'As many live because they are afraid to die, as die, because they are afraid to live.'[143] Such judgements are, however, highly questionable. Pain of any kind is subjective. We cannot know how much or how little suffering it has taken to make someone suicidal. It is not for us to judge. St Augustine argued that Lucrece ought not to have killed herself because she had been raped. 'Tush,' he said, 'another's lust cannot pollute thee.'[144] How, in the name of goodness, could *he* know?

Socrates was forced to drink hemlock. He had refused to agree to a plan that would enable him to escape from Athens to Thessaly, feeling it was his duty to stay and abide the death sentence. He argues strongly, however, against suicide. When asked by his friends why he considered suicide to be sacrilegious, he answers:

> Take for instance the parable told in the Mysteries about these matters, that men are placed in a kind of guard-post, and should neither release themselves from it, nor desert . . . I still believe that there is some truth in the idea that the gods are our guardians, and that we men are only part of the property which belongs to the gods.[145]

Pressed to strengthen his argument, he continues:

> . . . I am confident that something awaits us after death; and that
> is why I trust the tradition which says that whatever awaits us,
> it is something far better for the good man than for the evil man.[145]

The argument is not a very convincing one — unless, that is, one
believes in the Mysteries to which he referred. Notions of sin and
punishment in the afterlife were not, however, a significant feature
of the public religion of Greece. One is reminded of Immanuel
Kant's position on suicide. 'There is', he said, '*but one* categorical
imperative, which may be thus stated: Act in conformity with
that maxim, *and that maxim only*, which you can at the same
time will to be universal law' [my italics].[146] We can see that,
applying Kant's imperative, it must be wrong to steal, since if
everyone did likewise there would be nothing left to steal. Similarly
it is wrong to commit murder, because if everyone did so there
would be no one left for everyone to kill. It is not possible,
however, to prove suicide wrong by applying Kant's reasoning,
because it *would* be quite possible for someone, a melancholic
for example, to wish that everyone followed his lead in self-
destruction. Nevertheless, Kant *did* think that suicide was wrong,
an insult against our humanity. Ludwig Wittgenstein, in his
Notebooks,[147] said:

> If suicide is allowed then everything is allowed.
> If anything is not allowed then suicide is not allowed.
> This throws a light on the nature of ethics, for suicide is, so to
> speak, the elementary sin. And when one investigates it it is like
> investigating mercury vapour in order to comprehend the nature
> of vapours.
> Or is even suicide in itself neither good nor evil?

It seems that, like Socrates, neither Kant nor Wittgenstein could
offer a truly logical reason for saying that suicide is immoral.
'Suicide is wrong because suicide is wrong' is what Wittgenstein
seems to be saying. In fact the only reasons that seem to work
are based on our feelings or beliefs. Suicide is wrong because
we feel it is wrong or because we believe that it contravenes the
law of God or the gods.

Schopenhauer did not say that suicide was a crime. Rather he
saw it as an error. He condemned the 'vulgar bigotry that prevails
in England'[148] which imposed dishonour upon the remains of
those who had taken their own lives. He felt that no penalty could

in any case be effective against people who did not fear death itself. The error in suicide, Schopenhauer believed, lay in the fact that the release it afforded was only apparent. As Patrick Gardiner explains in his book on Schopenhauer,

> By killing himself the suicide assuredly brings to an end his existence as an empirical individual, as a particular phenomenon of will, and so destroys his individual consciousness 'which is bound to the individual body'. But it by no means follows therefrom that he destroys his metaphysical essence, since this lies 'outside time' and hence cannot be extinguished by any act undertaken against a merely phenomenal and therefore temporal objectification of its nature.[148]

Much influenced by Indian thought, Schopenhauer was of the opinion that the doctrine of transmigration, even if not literally true, contained truth in a mythological sense. Buddhist thought would not brand suicide a sin or a crime but rather as an example of 'unskilful means' — an error, as Schopenhauer put it. There is certainly something to be said in favour of this middle position, which answers 'yes' to Wittgenstein's question, 'is . . . suicide in itself neither good nor evil?' Perhaps it comes close to the attitude that seems to be emerging in our own time, the attitude which has led to the 1961 Suicide legislation.

There have, of course, been many attempts to justify suicide, to present it as an amoral act, if not a moral one. The philosophies of the Cynics, Stoics and Epicureans all led to an acceptance of suicide. Cynicism was founded by Diogenes, who decided to live like a dog (hence the name 'cynic', which means doglike), rejecting all conventions. He sought virtue and moral freedom, as the Buddhists do, by liberation from desire. Stoicism, founded by Zeno, a Cypriot, held that we are all part of a single system, nature, and that the good life was living in harmony with nature. Virtue was the main goal and so health, happiness and possessions were of no account. Among the adherents of Stoicism were the Spaniard, Seneca, and Epictetus, a Greek, both of whom have already been quoted in Chapter 8. The other great Stoic was the Emperor Marcus Aurelius, whose indifference to death was expressed in the following words from his *Meditations*: 'If a god were to tell you, "Tomorrow, or at best the day after, you will be dead," you would not, unless the most abject of men, be greatly solicitous whether it was to be the later day, rather than the morrow — for what is the difference between them?'[149] The third group, the Epicureans, named after their founder, Epicurus, regarded pleasure as 'the beginning and end of the blessed life'. Whatever caused pain was evil, and like the Stoics and Cynics they claimed to be indifferent to death.

Much nearer our own time the English poet, John Donne, wrote 'Biathanatos',[150] a defence of suicide. Published in 1646, fifteen years after his death, it contains the admission that he himself had contemplated suicide: '. . . whensoever any afflication assailes me, mee thinks I have the keyes of my prison in mine owne hand, and no remedy presents it selfe so soone to my heart, as mine own sword.' He concludes with a quotation from Ausonius, which he applies to death: 'Thou providest that thy benefits, and the good which thou bringest shall not be transitory; and that the ills from which thou deliverest us, shall never return.' Donne's purpose was to demonstrate that self-homicide was not 'so naturally a sin, that it may never be otherwise.' His approach is to examine the question of the morality of suicide from the viewpoints of natural law and of civil and ecclesiastical law; he comments on the texts from the Scriptures and the Fathers condemning suicide. Not surprisingly, in the light of the strength of the Church's antipathy towards the view he was presenting 'Biathanatos' displays as much defence as argument. It is almost as though Donne were continually looking over his shoulder.

Just over 130 years after the publication of Donne's treatise another defence was published, also posthumously. It was an essay, Of Suicide, and it was written by the Scottish philosopher, David Hume. With his customary logic, Hume produces some powerful arguments. A sceptic for whom God was 'a riddle, an enigma, an inexplicable mystery', he was unwilling to grant that the deity had any rational bearing on human destiny. Thus he is able to produce highly objective comments on the view promoted by Aquinas that suicide is an offence against God:

> Were the disposal of human life so much reserved as the peculiar province of the Almighty that it were an encroachment on his right, for men to dispose of their own lives; it would be equally criminal to act for the preservation of life as for its destruction. If I turn aside a stone which is falling upon my head, I disturb the course of nature, and I invade the peculiar province of the Almighty by lengthening out my life beyond the period which by the general laws of matter and motion he had assigned it.[151]

This illustrates how difficult it is for those who feel that suicide is wrong to adduce logical arguments in support of their case.

Even when the premise that God is in control of our lives is accepted, the immorality of suicide is difficult to prove. It is, of course, equally hard to make out a logically irrefutable case that suicide is right. One can defend self-destruction against the arguments advanced by its opponents, as Donne and Hume did. One can argue that suicide might be outside the categories of right and wrong, as Schopenhauer did. But *can* one make out a logical case for suicide as a rational act?

The idea of philosophical suicide has been examined by a number of authors. Among them was Dostoevsky. In his novel, *The Possessed*,[152] he describes why Kirillov, one of a group of five revolutionary conspirators, takes his own life. Kirillov, a structural engineer, is an atheist and, like Dostoevsky himself, an epileptic. And he is an advocate of logical suicide. For him suicide is the highest expression of self-will, a perfectly free action. His argument is absurd.

> If there is no God, then I am God . . . If God exists, all is His will and from His will I cannot escape. If not, it's all my will and I am bound to show self-will . . . I am bound to show my unbelief . . . I have no higher idea than disbelief in God. I have all the history of mankind on my side. Man has done nothing but invent God so as to go on living, and not kill himself . . . I am the first one in the whole history of mankind who would not invent God . . . the salvation for all consists in proving this idea to everyone . . . To recognise that there is no God and not to recognise at the same instant that one is God oneself is an absurdity, else one would certainly kill oneself. If you recognize it you are sovereign, and then you won't kill yourself but will live in the greatest glory. But one, the first, must kill himself, for else who will begin and prove it? So I must certainly kill myself, to begin and prove it.

And Kirillov kills himself. It is a futile act.

The poet, Mallarmé, was troubled for much of his life by thoughts of suicide. In his essay, 'Mallarmé: The Poetry of Suicide',[153] the existentialist philosopher, Jean-Paul Sartre, tells us that Mallarmé 'would have had to believe in God, for it was God who guaranteed Poetry'. But he no longer did. 'Mallarmé, a purely material creature', writes Sartre, 'sought to conjure up an order of existence superior to matter. His was a *theological* impotence: the death of God left a void which the poet tried to fill, and failed.' Quoting a passage from Flaubert in which St Anthony is tempted with the words, 'Do something which will make you the equal of God . . . He created you — and by the virtue of your courage, you are free to destroy his handiwork,' Sartre says that 'in Mallarmé's contemplated suicide there was an element of terrorist crime. And didn't he say once that suicide and crime were the only *supernatural* acts of which man was capable?' Later in the same essay Sartre goes on to say:

> To a greater degree than Nietzsche, he experienced the death of God; well before Camus, he felt that suicide was the original question confronting man; his struggle day after day against chance would be taken up later by others, yet with no greater lucidity. In a word, what he asked himself was this: Is there a way to be found within determinism that leads outside it? Is it possible to turn *praxis* upside-down and rediscover subjectivity by reducing the universe and oneself to objectivity?

Like Kirillov's argument this is false. Albert Camus, in the introduction to *The Rebel*,[154] puts his finger on the illogicality when, criticizing the stance of those who regard everything as being without meaning, that is absurd, he writes:

> If the world is a matter of indifference to the suicide, this is because he has an idea of something which is not or could not be indifferent to him. One thinks that one will destroy everything along with one; but from this very death a value arises which would, perhaps, have justified existence.

As Camus puts it elsewhere in the same Introduction, 'To say that life is absurd, one must be alive.' Kirillov's suicide proves nothing to those who are left, for there have been many suicides. The only person to whom it speaks is himself, and he would have to be alive for the idea of his suicide to have any meaning. Mallarmé's position is equally false. If he believes only in determinism how can his death lead *him* out of it? Dead, he has no subjectivity, only the objectivity he wishes to lose. The ideas of Kirillov and Mallarmé have meaning only for those who hold them. The attempt to prove them renders them meaningless.

Before leaving the question of the morality of suicide we must look at it from the viewpoint of the biologist. Is suicide of advantage to the species? Is man the only animal to kill itself? Now it can readily be argued that animals cannot commit suicide, for to do so would imply self-awareness coupled with will, the ability to have intention. In his essay, 'Can a Mouse Commit Suicide?',[155] Halmuth H. Schafer admits that we do not yet know. Durkheim is more definite in his comments on the subject:

Our knowledge of animal intelligence does not really allow us to attribute to them an understanding anticipatory of their death nor, especially, of the means to accomplish it. Some, to be sure, are known to refuse to enter a spot where others have been killed; they seem to have a presentiment of death. Actually, however, the smell of blood sufficiently explains this instinctive reaction. All cases cited at all authentically which might appear true suicides may be quite differently explained.[6]

Stengel supports this view: 'Nobody has proved that the faithful dog who starves to death on his master's grave knows that the master is dead, nor is there any evidence that the lemmings, which plunge into the sea to their death, do so from an urge to self-destruction.'[68] From the biologist's point of view, however, it does not really matter whether the self-destructive behaviour is knowingly altruistic. It would be enough to find examples of a naturally self-destructive activity which in some way helps to preserve the species.

And, of course, there *are* some. Richard Dawkins, in his book, *The Selfish Gene*,[156] argues that the apparent altruism found throughout nature results from the *selfishness* of genes. Life forms, plants, animals, insects and so on, are in his view *survival machines* to ensure the continuance of the genes that created them. Thus all animal behaviour may have a part to play in the preservation of the genes, the replicators. Dawkins cites the 'Kamikaze' behaviour of worker bees, which will sting intruders to the hive and die as a result. He observes that 'suicide in the interests of caring for other individuals is incompatible with future bearing of one's own offspring,' and that 'suicidal self-sacrifice therefore seldom evolves.'

> But a worker bee never bears offspring of its own. All its efforts are directed to preserving its genes by caring for relatives other than its own offspring. The death of a single sterile worker bee is no more serious to its genes than is the shedding of a leaf in autumn to the genes of a tree.

In language that is reminiscent of Eugène Marais's book, *The Soul of the White Ant*,[157] he asserts that:

> A society of ants, bees, or termites achieves a kind of individuality at a higher level. Food is shared to such an extent that one may speak of a communal stomach. Information is shared so efficiently by chemical signals and by the famous 'dance' of the bees that the community behaves almost as if it were a unit with a nervous

· system and sense organs of its own. Foreign intruders are recognized and repelled with something of the selectivity of a body's immune reaction system. The rather high temperature inside a beehive is regulated nearly as precisely as that of the human body, even though an individual bee is not a 'warm blooded' animal. Finally and most importantly, the analogy extends to reproduction. The majority of individuals in a social insect colony are sterile workers. The 'germ line' — the line of immortal gene continuity — flows through the bodies of a minority of individuals, the reproductives. These are the analogues of our own reproductive cells in our testes and ovaries. The sterile workers are the analogy of our liver, muscle, and nerve cells.

By a stretch of the imagination one might be able to discern a parallel between the suicidal behaviour of worker bees and Durkheim's model of human suicide as result of purely social influences. The social insect's actions are instinctive; they are programmed to benefit the community. Quoting Dr Bugnion of the University of Lausanne, who studied the behaviour of termites in Ceylon, Eugène Marais writes: 'the multifarious duties, which are carried out under our eyes by the soldiers on the one hand and the workers on the other, give us the illusion of a higher direction, whereas in reality this direction does not exist, or if it does exist resides solely in the community as a whole.'[157] Marais's book, *The Soul of the White Ant*, was first published in 1937. Forty years earlier, Durkheim, writing of human behaviour, tells us that:

> the social suicide-rate can be explained only sociologically. At any given moment the moral constitution of society establishes the contingent of voluntary deaths. There is, therefore, for each people a collective force of a definite amount of energy, impelling man to self-destruction. The victim's acts which at first seem to express only his personal temperament are really the supplement and prolongation of a social condition which they express externally.[6]

Durkheim's model of suicidal behaviour in human society does seem to bear some resemblance to the ant-hill and the beehive, and it is not difficult to find examples to illustrate the analogy. When, for example, a human society is threatened, say, by war, it organizes itself in a such a way that its individual members display, or are expected to display, the same kind of altruistic behaviour we think we see in the beehive and ant-hill. There is, however, one fundamental difference which must lead us to question both the altruism of social insects and Durkheim's model of suicide. No one put it more compellingly than did Blaise Pascal:

Man is but a reed, the weakest in nature; but he is a thinking reed.
It does not take the whole Universe in arms to crush him. A vapour,
a drop of water is enough to kill him. But if the Universe were
to crush him, man would still be nobler than his killer. *For he
knows that he is dying*, and that the Universe has the advantage
over him; the Universe knows nothing of this [my italics].[108]

It is only humans who can ask, 'Whose life is it anyway?'.[158]

10.

WHAT THEN SHALL WE DO?

To whom shall I speak today?
  I am laden with misery
  through lack of an intimate.

Anon, *A Dispute Over Suicide*, Egypt, before 2000 BC

Among the many points that have emerged in this brief, but wide-ranging survey of suicide there are a few that have special bearing on the approach to be taken for avoidance or prevention. Let us recap. First, whatever the origin of suicidal action, whether it be mental disturbance or depression or external circumstances, the victim will have felt that he had good reason for the course he took. From his point of view it will not have been an aimless act. There will have been a purpose: some problem to be solved, some pain, mental or physical or perhaps both, to be brought to an end, a situation from which to escape. There will have been in the constricted thinking of the victim some compelling logic and an apparent lack of any viable or acceptable alternative to self-destruction. Secondly, there will have been some ambivalence in his attitude, some conflict between the will to live and the desire to die. However logical the reasoning has seemed to be, there may have been some strange double-think, a desire to die and yet at the same time not to be dead. In fact it may have been that there was no wish for death but only for an end to, or even an interruption in, awareness, feeling or consciousness, in a word: cessation. And thirdly there will have been a possibly growing sense of isolation. We saw in our references to the work of Durkheim and Halbwachs how the social and psychological influences that favoured suicidal thoughts and actions were those which separated the individual from the intimacy of others. The suicide victim may not have been alone but he is likely to have felt lonely or at least to have had some area of his life which he has been unable to disclose or share. This is not to say, of course, that people who keep things to themselves are likely to become suicidal — far from it; but when deep unhappiness remains unshared and the individual becomes increasingly withdrawn from the world and his thinking is more and more centred upon himself, suicide becomes a real possibility. When ambivalence recedes and thinking becomes constricted to the point where no alternative to suicide is thought possible the risk is high. At such moments the thought can become an urge, the idea an act. At such moments intervention may be impracticable and, from the victim's standpoint, undesirable. The state of mind may be such that the possibility that anyone can, or indeed should, have concern for his fate is wholly inconceivable.

What should one do when one is assailed by thoughts of suicide? The answer, strangely, is to do what many suicidal people do almost automatically: tell someone. It is perhaps surprising but nevertheless true that a great many people who are considering suicide seek to communicate their intention to those around them. They may do this quite deliberately or they may do so inadvertently. Unfortunately, for reasons which have been discussed, the signals are often not picked up. Often it is because of the old fallacy that people who talk about suicide never actually do anything about it. Often it is because the references to suicide are too oblique for them to be picked up by friends and colleagues and it is only after the event that the significance of the allusions is recognized. So the message to anyone who is plagued by thoughts of suicide is, yes, tell someone, but make sure that the person to whom the disclosure is made is someone who *will* understand. Who might such a person be? One obvious possibility is the family doctor. Not only will he treat revelations of suicidal feelings as serious, but he will hear them in confidence, as he does all personal information given him by patients. He can help by counselling, by referral to a psychologist or psychiatrist, or by the prescription of such drugs as may be appropriate. There are, however, problems for the doctor. Although it is known that about two-thirds of those who commit a parasuicidal act have consulted a general practitioner within a month before the event, by no means all will have given clear indications of suicidal inclinations. The time the patient has with the doctor may not be sufficient for the delicate subject to be brought into the open.

Another problem for the general practitioner is that he cannot always be available when his patient is feeling suicidal. Doctors are well aware that this is so and that it should nevertheless be possible for their patients to be able to speak to someone at such moments. Thus in a report published by the Royal College of General Practitioners [159] the following recommendation is made:

> Potentially suicidal patients should be given a telephone number which they can ring at any time of the day or night if suicidal feelings become overwhelming. This may be the practice number or that of a voluntary organisation such as the local Samaritan group.

This brings us to the other obvious contact which might be made by the person who is feeling suicidal: the Samaritans. Often the individual who is beset by thoughts of suicide finds it too embarrassing to speak about them. There is no *reason* why this should be so. We have no reservations about sharing with others that we are suffering from a cold or that we have had an abysmal holiday or that we are afraid of thunderstorms. But to speak directly about suicide, especially in the context of our own possible self-destruction, is not something we undertake lightly. Thus it may be that it is easier to speak of such matters to someone who remains unseen and anonymous, someone who does not and *need* not know who it is that is feeling suicidal. The ability to telephone an understanding and anonymous person at any time of the day or night and to speak in confidence, *total* confidence, must be of value. It should also be easy and unthreatening to telephone such a person, since the caller has it in his power to terminate the call at any time and to remain anonymous throughout. Even so, people still find it hard to open a conversation that may lead to discussion of their deeper feelings. It is not surprising, therefore, that those who offer to listen to the suicidal on the telephone are familiar with the call that ends before a word has been said, with the caller who remains silent for a period before saying anything or before replacing the receiver, with the trivial excuse for calling, the call that purports to seek information but in fact has been made with the purpose of talking about feelings. None of this is in any way remarkable. Even in the happiest of circumstances we find it difficult to open conversation with strangers and we devise stratagems for doing so: we speak about the weather, which allows us to make contact without the formality of an introduction; it is a neutral topic which can lead to or circumvent conversation. Anyone who wishes to speak about suicidal feelings to a member of an organization such as the Samaritans (of which more later) need have no qualms about how to open the conversation. Remember that the person receiving the call is *expecting* to be approached and understands the hesitation of the caller. There is no need to justify the call. All that need be said is: 'I would like to speak to someone,' or 'I am feeling pretty depressed,' or even a candid statement such as 'I don't know where to begin.' The person at the other end *wants* to hear you speak and is trained to help you do so.

What good will it do to speak to someone about suicidal feelings? The person whose misery has reached the stage where suicide seems a possible way out or the only way out understandably believes that neither he nor anyone else, especially anyone else, can change the way he feels. 'There is nothing anyone can do. So why bother?' There may be a kind of perverse notion that nobody could conceivably be concerned with the victim's fate and that if anyone *were* concerned it would merely confirm the victim's sense of his own inadequacy and worthlessness: 'I am pitiable and I don't want pity.' The simple answer is that suicide is an irrevocable step and should not be taken until all possible alternatives have been explored. After all, what is there to lose? The Voluntary Euthanasia Society, who believe that people have the right to choose the time and manner of their death, are at pains to make this point. This most serious of all decisions, to end one's own life, should never be taken without careful and informed consideration of the alternatives, and this means talking to someone not directly involved in the problem, whatever that may be. Of course no one can *persuade* the suicidal person to change his mind. No one can provide a reason for living. No one can transform circumstances. What they *can* do is listen and support. It is astonishing how often merely talking about one's feelings can help. Many people go through life ignoring or suppressing their feelings. They find it difficult to speak about how they feel and they need help to do so. The act of talking about feelings allows the individual to develop a new perspective towards them. Often the attempt to articulate how he feels leads him to a new understanding of his predicament. Sharing suicidal feelings with another person may be the first step in breaking out of a closed pattern of thinking. Talking can soothe agitated feelings. Most importantly, talking is a way out of the sense of isolation that so many suicidal people have. The relationship between speaker and listener can provide the support that is needed for moments of crisis to be passed and survived.

One of the major shortcomings of our society is that we do not listen to each other. We *hear* what is being said to us but we are not *listening*. To convert hearing into listening we have to add attention. How often does one hear the complaint: 'You're not listening' and the response 'Oh yes I am,' followed by a recitation of the last few sentences spoken, with a view to proving that listening has in fact taken place. But it hasn't and the recitation serves only to cause anger. The complainant is usually right: there has been a lack of attention. We mean to listen, but we are thwarted by our own thoughts. 'I am fed up,' says Joan to Fred. Fred immediately starts thinking about what might be making her feel that way instead of waiting attentively to hear from her why she is fed up. Or he thinks, 'Here we go again, the same old story,' even though there is no reason to believe that it *is* the same old story. And in any case, since he probably wasn't listening the last time either, he really has no idea what the old story was. Or he thinks, '*She's* fed up — what about me?' and before Joan knows what has happened to her she is drawn into a conversation about *his* fed-up feelings. Or he thinks, 'As soon as she has finished telling me about what has made her feel fed up I shall have to say something helpful — I wonder what I can say'; in other words Fred is deafened by what he is going to say next. Often you can hear two people talking to each other *simultaneously*, each transmitting on full power, neither receiving at all. One of the great enemies of listening is the fact that silence embarrasses us, causing us to act promptly to abolish it by making comments, relevant or otherwise; the result, however, is that the words the speaker's pause has been aimed at finding are lost for ever. Silence is no problem for those whose feelings are shared. Lovers can tolerate long periods of silence when they are together. But when the feelings are not shared and there is a need to listen attentively, to await the spoken word, we speak rather than listen. I cannot help thinking that if we spoke less and paid more attention to each other there might be a beneficial effect on the suicide rate.

Paying attention is not just a matter of listening to the stories we are told. Often it is much more important to be aware of how a person is feeling than to hear what he is saying. In other words our aim should be empathy. The Oxford Dictionary defines empathy as 'the power of entering into the experience of or understanding objects or emotions outside ourselves'. I prefer the definition offered by the great American authority on non-directive counselling, Carl Rogers. It is 'being sensitive, moment to moment, to the changing felt meanings which flow in [the] other person'.[160] If each suicidal person were to be surrounded by empathetic neighbours would his sense of isolation not be overcome? It is a tall order to ask that we all become empathizers. One might as well ask that everyone becomes a saint. 'Thou shalt love thy neighbour as thyself,' says the scripture. It is a virtue commended by all the great religions: charity. Many seek to acquire it, only to find that neighbours are not always very lovable. The gap between theory and practice is a big one. As Chesterton said,

> I learned with little labour
> The way to love my fellow-man
> And hate my next-door neighbour.[161]

Perhaps the first step to charity, to loving one's neighbour, is to pay attention to him.

It is a natural and commendable feature of people's desire to help their neighbours that they should wish to do so in a positive and practical way. Often such an approach is the most appropriate. The way to help an elderly or blind person who clearly wishes to cross the road is to lead him by the hand. Helping the suicidal, however, is a different matter. Any action which seems to take responsibility from the suicidal person may serve only to deepen the sense of guilt and inadequacy that is the source of his unhappiness. We may help him to find a way out of his predicament or to develop a life-affirming attitude but the thinking that has to take place must be his own. Only he can change his mind. Alexander Solzhenitsyn examines the question of the individual's need for self-determination in his novel, *Cancer Ward*.[162] The patient, Kostoglotov has gone to see his doctor, Ludmila Afanasyevna Dontsova. They have a lengthy conversation. Kostoglotov finds communication difficult:

> Wasn't that typical of life? Here, sitting in front of him, was his compatriot, his contemporary and well-wisher. They were talking in their own language, common to them both, and still he couldn't explain the simplest thing to her. It seemed one had to start too far back, or else end the explanation too soon.

Their discussion is about the nature of his treatment; it is an argument which the doctor wins. At one point comes the following dialogue.

'You will go home,' Dontsova weighed her words one by one with great emphasis, 'when I consider it necessary to interrupt your treatment. And then you will only go temporarily.'

Kostoglotov had been waiting for this moment in the conversation. He couldn't let it go by without a fight.

'Ludmila Afanasyevna! Can't we get away from this tone of voice? You sound like a grown-up talking to a child. Why not talk as an adult to an adult? Seriously, when you were on your rounds this morning I . . . '

'Yes, on my rounds this morning' — Dontsova's big face looked quite threatening — 'you made a disgraceful scene. What are you trying to do? Upset the patients? What are you putting into their heads?'

'What was I trying to do?' He spoke without heat but emphatically, as Dontsova had. He sat up, his back firm against the back of the chair. 'I simply wanted to remind you of my right to dispose of my own life. A man can dispose of his own life, can't he? You agree I have that right?'

Dontsova looked down at his colourless, winding scar and was silent. Kostoglotov developed his point:

'You see, you start from a completely false position. No sooner does a patient come to you than you begin to do all his thinking for him. After that, the thinking's done by your standing orders, your five-minute conferences, your programme, your plan and the honour of your medical department. And once again I become a grain of sand, just like I was in the camp. Once again nothing *depends* on me.'

There are two points here. One is to do with the ethics of intervention, to which we shall return later. The other is the matter of the individual's feelings — Kostoglotov's sense of being no more than a grain of sand. It is, for the suicide counsellor, a question of respect for the individual; it is also of cardinal importance in determining the outcome of his counselling. The person being counselled must in the end *want* to stay alive. The fact that the counsellor wants him to reject his suicidal thoughts is relevant to him only to the extent that it plays a part in the development of the kind of relationship he needs. 'I want you to live' means 'I am interested in you; I care what happens to you', nothing more, but it is enough.

Whatever the logic employed by the suicidal to justify their acts of self-destruction, the decisions they reach are, at the deepest level, a matter of how they *feel*. Instinctively we know that this is so, and yet, faced with someone who says 'I want to kill myself,' our natural instinct is to attempt to persuade him not to do it. In Racine's play, *Phaedra*,[163] the Queen's nurse and confidante, Oenone, advances the kinds of argument that anyone might be tempted to use.* Phaedra, the wife of Theseus, King of Athens, has an overpowering infatuation for her stepson, Hyppolytus. Half demented with guilt, she is close to suicide. Oenone argues fiercely:

> Deaf to our wild entreaties, pitiless,
> Will you allow yourself to perish thus?
> What madness cuts you off in mid career?
> What spell, what poison, has dried up the source?
> Thrice have the shades of night darkened the skies
> Since sleep last made its entry in your eyes,
> And thrice the day has driven forth dim night
> Since last your fainting lips took nourishment.
> What dark temptation lures you to your doom?
> What right have you to plot to end your life?
> In this you wrong the gods from whom you spring,
> You are unfaithful to your wedded lord;
> Unfaithful also to your hapless sons,
> Whom you would thrust beneath a heavy yoke.

This line of argument having no effect, Oenone tries another tack, one which many a would-be suicide must have heard:

> Keep silence then, inhuman one, and die;
> But seek some other hand to close your eyes.
> Although the candle of your life burns low,
> I will go down before you to the dead.
> Thither a thousand different roads converge,
> My misery will choose the shortest one.
> When have I ever failed you, cruel one?
> Remember, you were born into my arms.
> For you I have lost country, children, all.
> Is this how you reward fidelity?'

Such entreaties seldom succeed and nor do these. Phaedra lives awhile, long enough to curse Oenone — 'You meddling fool!' — but dies from self-administered poison, believing that

> '. . . death, robbing my eyes of light, will give
> Back to the sun its tarnished purity.'

---

* In Sophocles' play, *Ajax*, Tecmessa tries similar arguments on Ajax — in vain. (See *Electra and Other Plays*, translated by E. F. Watling, Penguin Books, 1984.)

Another line of argument that many seek to employ boils down to what must seem almost an accusation to the suicidal person: 'I have been through the crisis you are now undergoing and *I* survived; so can you.' Although it is well meant, such an approach can be counterproductive. The success it recalls merely polarizes the sense of failure felt by the victim. 'It's alright for people like you, but I'm not able to cope.' And to feelings of inadequacy are added those of guilt. This is a danger inherent in the kind of counselling that might be offered by some of those self-help organizations set up by the survivors of traumatic experiences to give support to those who have not yet recovered. Such organizations can be invaluable in providing companionship, understanding, information and practical help, but it is important that those who offer such services are trained in non-directive counselling.

Those of us who are fortunate enough to find life worthwhile — the vast majority of us — usually have little difficulty in listing what makes life so attractive. Although we may have no desire to live for ever, we are never too keen on the idea of an early departure. We can always think of a good reason why we should still be here tomorrow. We should never think, however, that we can enthuse the suicidal with such reasons. As James Thomson said,

> Speak not of comfort where no comfort is,
>   Speak not at all: can words make foul things fair?
>   . . . for words must shrink from the most wordless woes.[29]

Our reasons for wanting to survive are our own. They may have much to do with other people but no one gives them to us. All that anyone can do is to help us find our *own raison d'être*, our own motivation. No one can *persuade* us to want to live; they can only help us to convince ourselves that we do. When we speak to the suicidal, therefore, it serves no purpose to tell them what makes life worthwhile for us. All we achieve by doing so is to sharpen the contrast between their feelings and ours.

Similarly, there is no advantage in offering advice. When we advise someone on a course of action we think he might take, what we are really saying is 'If I were in your shoes . . ', which is patently not the case. Moreover, by proffering advice we are implying that we are wiser than the person himself: we know how to cope and he does not. The chances are, in any case, that the advice we would give is inappropriate, either because it has already been considered and rejected or because we have an incomplete understanding of the person's circumstances and of the way in which he would feel comfortable to react to them. Publilius Syrus summed it up in the first century BC when he said, 'Many receive advice, few profit by it.'[164] It might be said, of course, that many distressed people seem to be crying out for someone to tell them what to do. Perhaps, but it is still unwise to advise them. There are two reasons for this. First, the advice may in the event turn out to have been bad and you will be held responsible for the consequences; and moreover you will now be in no good position to offer further help. Secondly, if the advice proves to have been good, you will have begun to establish dependence when what is desperately needed is the very opposite, the ability to make mature, effective decisions independently.

So, we do not give advice. We do not take the individual's decisions for him. What, then, do we do? We listen. The most helpful thing we can say is, 'Tell me.' And when the telling starts we must listen with all our attention focused on the person. We can encourage further talk by reflecting back what we hear the person say. Hearing what he has said may give him a new perspective. It will also help by conveying to him that someone understands. It is no good saying, 'I know how you feel'; who in his right mind could believe that? But, by reflecting, by listening and by gentle encouragement to talk we can show that we are involved. We can begin to establish a caring, receptive relationship which eases his sense of isolation. We do not react adversely to anything we are told, nor do we express anything that might be taken for pity — what *we* feel is probably of little importance in any case. And we must not shy away from the subject of suicide. In fact, if it does not come into the open we should raise it ourselves, but gently so that the individual does not feel a desire to deny his suicidal thoughts rather than speak of what causes his alarm or makes him feel guilty.

People who undertake the role of counsellor are often most reluctant to bring the conversation round to the subject of suicide. There are several reasons why they may be hesitant about doing so. First, it is often felt that by mentioning it we might put the idea into someone's head. Perhaps by showing that we are not shocked by the thought of suicide we may make it seem more acceptable. Reflection, however, should reassure us. Suicide is not the sort of notion that enters one's head casually. To put it bluntly, one is unlikely to say of suicide, 'I hadn't thought of that before; I shall consider it.' The view expressed in a report published by the Royal College of General Practitioners is that 'there should never be any hesitation in asking any agitated or depressed patient if he has wanted to kill himself'.[159] My own experience is that frequently when I have brought the subject of suicide into a counselling conversation it has been greeted with relief and there has then been a willingness to talk about it. Where there have been no thoughts of suicide the response has been quite matter-of-fact. Only very rarely have I been asked why I raised the subject.

Other reasons for our dislike of introducing the subject of suicide into conversation are to do with our fear of being unable to cope with the response it evokes. Some of this fear arises because we dislike the prospect of sharing the distressing emotions that may be released and some is caused by our anxiety about the kind of response that might be expected of us. However ill-founded such fears may be, they are understandable. We have been brought up in a society where strong emotions are suppressed and where such expressions of unhappiness as do occur are to be met with constructive sympathy. Consequently we are embarrassed when someone admits to suicidal feelings, and we do not know what to say. We may also be discomfited because we are not sure that our own belief systems and our attitudes to our own mortality can withstand the kind of confrontation that talking about someone else's suicidal feelings entails. To cope with these negative feelings we need training and support, to which reference will be made in the next chapter. For the present, we must recognize that confrontation with suicidal feelings *will* be demanding. There will be a run on one's emotional resources, but the more one can focus one's attention on the *other* person's feelings rather than on one's own, the better will one be able to contain it. The better, too, will one be able to respond, for the best response is to attend, to help the other person to express his feelings, to help *him* overcome his sense of isolation, his lack of an intimate.

11.

SUICIDE PREVENTION

> He felt the enormous relief of speaking without prudence to
> someone who, he believed, understood him . . . encouraged him
> to lay down for a short time the burden of secrecy.
>
> Graham Greene, *The Human Factor*

Some will ask if it is right to intervene with a view to preventing
suicide. 'He who saves a man against his will as good as murders
him,'[165] said the Roman satirist and poet, Horace. One can respect
the argument. If we can be sure the victim is out of his senses
it is reasonable to strive to protect him from himself. But, since
many people who attempt suicide show no signs of psychological
disturbance other than the act itself, we must judge them to be
of sound mind and then it is debatable whether we have any right
to interfere with their plans. There is no clear case which all would
accept. Those who have certain religious convictions may believe
that it is right to strive to prevent the commission of a mortal
sin. In the days when suicide was treated as a felony we should
have been well within our rights to interfere with a view to
preventing a crime. (As recently as 1950 the Chairman of a
Magistrates Court, giving a six months prison sentence to a woman
for making a second suicide attempt, told her, 'You have been
here before and we gave you every opportunity to go straight.')
But what do we do now when the law places no such
responsibility upon us and we do not have any clear religious
guidance? Each must decide for himself. I have a strong inclination
towards the view that every one of us is responsible for his own
life and should be given maximum freedom to dispose of it as
he wishes. Yet, if I saw someone embarking upon some activity
which I knew to carry a high probability of fatal injury, would
I not be perfectly justified in warning him, even in restraining

him until I was sure that he was aware of the risk he was about to take? If I can answer 'yes' to this question, should I not also deem it right to restrain someone from suicide, knowing as I do that there is a high probability that his suicidal urge is only temporary? Should I not also take account of my knowledge that there is likely to be an element of ambivalence in his thinking? If we see someone suffering the pangs of indecision do we not consider it reasonable to help by making sure that he has all the information he needs to make up his mind? Should I not, therefore, attempt to ensure that the suicidal person has been able to consider all the alternative ways of dealing with his unhappy circumstances? On the other hand, how hard should I strive to make someone reconsider his intention to kill himself when I know that every moment he lives is an agony for him?

The moral dilemma of whether one should intervene to forestall suicide is in the end a matter of which takes precedence in our thinking: life or liberty. Is life something sacred and suicide an obscenity? Or do we take a pragmatic view of life as being worth living only so long as it serves some purpose and of suicide as being something sensible one does in certain circumstances? And what do we make of liberty? Is every one of us to be master of his fate, captain of his soul? Or do we feel like the saintly brother of Father Zossima in Dostoevsky's *The Brothers Karamazov* that 'everyone of us is responsible for everyone else in every way'?[59] Perhaps in maintaining that no one can make these judgements for another person, that each of us must find his own answer, I am revealing a preference for liberty. Maybe so, but I am uncertain, for there could be circumstances in which my instinctive behaviour would be in contradiction to these considerations. Take, for example, a hypothetical situation. I am sitting in the sand-dunes behind a beach, reading *Cancer Ward*. I have reached the chapter where the patient Kostoglotov is arguing with Dontsova, the doctor:

'Why do you assume you have the right to decide for someone else? Don't you agree it's a terrifying right, one that rarely leads to good? You should be careful. No-one's entitled to it, not even doctors.'

It occurs to me that Kostoglotov is right, but my attention is suddenly caught by a strange spectacle. It is a man walking along the deserted beach in a dejected way. He does not notice that I am there. As I watch him he turns deliberately towards the sea and starts walking into the surf. What an odd thing to do, I think; he hasn't taken any of his clothes off, not even his shoes. Then it becomes clear: he is going to drown himself. I leap to my feet, dropping *Cancer Ward* in the sand, and I rush to the water's edge, shouting to the man to come back, but he does not hear. Already he is out of his depth and swimming steadily out beyond the waves. I cannot hope to reach him. Frantically I look round for help — a boat, someone else, but I am alone. I start running to the row of houses at the end of the beach. It is not yet too late. The man is only a speck on the sea but he is still swimming. I enter the telephone box and dial 999. 'Get me the Coastguards, please. It's urgent ... '

In point of fact the scenario described above would present no dilemma. Anyone confronted with someone whose life was in danger, whether through accidental circumstances or apparently deliberate self-destructive action, would take preventive steps. Whatever our views about the self-determinative rights of the individual we feel that suicide must remain a private act. I may condone suicide in certain circumstances but I cannot co-operate in it. This, of course, is what the law demands. The Suicide Act, 1961, abrogated previous legislation which made it a crime to take one's own life. It remains a criminal offence, however, to aid, abet, counsel or procure the suicide of another person. Anyone who assists another person to commit suicide is liable to be charged with murder, attempted murder or manslaughter and could receive life imprisonment. The offence of assisting suicide carries a maximum penalty of fourteen years in prison. Of course, being aware that someone might commit suicide does not imply co-operation. No one can be expected to assume the responsibility for ensuring that someone does not kill himself. But prevention is a worthwhile aim not at all in conflict with the freedom of the individual. I may wish to dissuade people from smoking, for example. I can do this by making sure that they are aware of the disadvantages of smoking. I can employ persuasion techniques to discourage them. I can, if I am in government, make tobacco expensive to buy. I can even ban smoking in certain places, saying in effect that no one shall smoke in my presence. But I am not forbidding smoking. The individual is still free to smoke.

Suicide prevention is probably a misnomer. Just as the Government could not prevent smoking without draconian measures so we could not prevent suicide without total surveillance of all potential victims. Suicide reduction would be a more accurate term but, since it is common to refer to *suicide prevention agencies*, I shall continue to do so. Perhaps the earliest prevention agency was The Parish of All Strangers founded in New York by the Revd Harry M. Warren in 1905 and renamed the National Save-A-Life League in the following year. 1906 also saw the establishment by the Salvation Army of The London Antisuicide Department. It was not until 1953, however, that the first steps were taken that resulted in the world-wide organization known as Befrienders International. The parent organization, The Samaritans, began in London. Its founder was the Revd Chad Varah, an Anglican priest. In 1935 as a newly ordained cleric he had to bury the body of a 14-year-old girl who had killed herself when her menstruation started. She had not known what was happening to her and had no one to ask about it. Chad resolved to do what he could to prevent other such tragic events and he began to give talks to youngsters and later to young couples about to be married. He had the idea that there ought to be an emergency telephone number for potential suicides and that they should thereby have access to someone with whom they could talk or, if they preferred, whom they could meet or with whom they could correspond. He was able to put his plan into action when he was appointed to St Stephen Walbrook in the City of London. He publicized the availability of the service he planned to offer by speaking to the journalists of Fleet Street. The *Daily Mirror* called it a 'Samaritan' service and the organization was born. Very soon Chad became aware that he could not cope with all the calls that were coming in unless he and his colleague, a former secretary who had agreed to help, had some assistance. At first he gathered together a group of helpers whose job it was to give tea or coffee and a listening ear to callers waiting to see him. He quickly realized that these helpers were performing a useful function beyond his expectations: many of the callers found that talking to his sympathetic volunteers was helpful to them. The rest is history. After the formation of the first Samaritan Branch in London came many others and now there are 180 in the British Isles with 20,000 volunteers. Everyone in these Islands has reasonable access to a Samaritan Branch. Chad's idea has spread to all corners of the world and now Befrienders International has branches from Sweden to New Zealand, from Brazil to Japan.

How worthwhile has it all been? How do we measure the benefits? One obvious measure of success would be the demand for the service the Samaritans offer. 'Good counsellors lack no clients,' said Shakespeare,* and the Samaritans have certainly not lacked callers in search of a sympathetic ear and the kind of non-directive counselling they provide. The number of calls taken by the Samaritans has increased dramatically since the Movement began in 1953 and is now over 2 million each year. The number of new callers in 1974 was 192,300. Ten years later, in 1984, it was double this figure, 358,500 new callers in the year. That is equivalent to something in the region of one new caller from one family in forty. Not all these callers are suicidal. Although in the mind of the public the Samaritans are linked with suicide, potential callers are wisely reminded in the Organization's publicity that they don't have to be suicidal to call the Samaritans. There is good reason for believing, however, that somewhere between one in three and one in two callers have given some serious thought to the possibility of taking their own lives. One would expect, therefore, that the Samaritans must have had some effect on the suicide rate. If this were so, then there could be no question that the Movement had been wholly worthwhile.

It is always difficult to *prove* anything from purely statistical evidence and many Samaritans would be satisfied with their own experience of callers whose intentions had been suicidal but who did not die and who attributed their survival to having been befriended when their spirits were low. The statistical evidence, however, is also strong (Diagram 3). In the years when the number of Samaritan branches was increasing there was a steady decline in the suicide rate which was not echoed in other countries where no such organization existed. Between 1963, when there were only 41 branches, and 1975, by which time the number of branches had risen to 165, the suicide rate for England and Wales dropped from 12.2 to 7.5 per 100,000 of the population. In other words there were in England and Wales in 1963 well over 5,500 suicides, while in 1975 there were well under 4,000. The year 1963 saw the highest number of suicides since before World War II and the decline from then until 1975 was fairly steady, as was the growth in Samaritan branches. This decline represents a significant saving of life. It is also quite unrepresentative of what was happening in most other countries over the same period. A study carried out for the World Health Organization [166] showed that of eighteen countries examined fifteen showed an *increase*

---

* *Measure for Measure.*

in the suicide rate between the early Sixties and the early Seventies. The exceptions were Scotland, with a fall of 3 per cent, Greece with a fall of 21 per cent and England and Wales with a fall of 34 per cent over the period considered. In some of the other fifteen countries the increase in their suicide rate over the corresponding period was more than 30 per cent. There is no proven explanation for the exceptionally high decline in England and Wales. That it is partly if not wholly due to the influence of the Samaritans is at least a plausible hypothesis. There have been objections to it, but no one has produced a satisfactory alternative. Nor has anyone produced an effective alternative approach to suicide prevention.

If we feel that we cannot accept the positive evidence for the effectiveness of the Samaritan approach perhaps we might consider it from the opposite point of view: why should it not work? Dr Richard Fox, who has made valuable contributions to suicide prevention on both sides of the Atlantic, made the following comment in his presentation to a conference on suicide held in New York in 1981; speaking of the discomfort felt by therapists when confronted by the expression of suicidal thoughts, he said:

> Yet for a suicidal person to reveal this deep, dark secret can be as cathartic as the proverbial lancing of an abscess. To do so anonymously, to someone who is 'outside the family' as it were, and to be accepted in loving and non-judgemental fashion, may make this positively life-preserving. Guilt can kill, but *shame* can kill equally.[167].

There is in the image presented here, the revelation of a deep, dark secret, a suggestion of the confessional. And in a sense this is precisely what the Samaritans provide: the possibility of disclosing without risk and anonymously the deepest and darkest of secrets. Through the medium of the telephone the suicidal person can speak with an intimacy that is almost certainly not available elsewhere. Few, if any, professional therapists can offer such a context. Inevitably the professional works in a relationship with his client which has, to begin with at any rate, a measure of formality. It is a doctor–patient relationship. For the Samaritan's caller there is from the outset the possibility of a warm, accepting relationship unhindered by real or imagined rules of behaviour. No subject is barred. No anxiety is too trivial to be discussed, no secret too awful to be shared.

The Samaritans have seven principles. The first of these is a statement of their objective:

*The primary aim of The Samaritans is to be available at any hour
of the day or night to befriend those passing through personal
crises and in imminent danger of taking their own lives.*

Availability is an essential feature of any suicide prevention agency.
For the suicidal it is important, perhaps crucial, that help is there
when they feel that way. For the despairing person alone at night
with the means of killing himself it is small comfort to know that
help will be available when morning comes or when the weekend
is over or when there is a gap in his doctor's diary. His need is
now. The morning may be too late or unbearably far away. Being
available means being there when you're needed. Throughout
the British Isles it is possible to contact a Samaritan branch at all
times, if not in one's own town then in a neighbouring one. It
is possible, too, to visit a branch during day hours or to write.
Many people have said that the mere knowledge that there was
someone there who could be contacted if they became desperate
was a source of comfort, a means of warding off panic.

The second of the seven principles says that:

*The Samaritans also seek to alleviate human misery, loneliness,
despair and depression by listening to and befriending those who
feel that they have no one else to turn to who would understand
and accept them.*

Being suicidal is an extension or consequence of feeling miserable,
lonely, despairing and depressed. It is such feelings that may make
suicide seem a possible course of action and perhaps, with the
passage of time, apparently the *only* course left. It is sensible,
therefore, for those suffering from them to seek help before
suicidal thoughts arise. Many, possibly 50 per cent or more, of
the Samaritans' callers do so, not infrequently saying, 'I'm not
suicidal, but . . . ' They are wise. It is good that they start early
to look for constructive ways of dealing with their unhappiness.
From the viewpoint of the helping agency whose first priority
is to save life there is a desire also to support those who are
dispirited. Both objectives are worthy and in many instances they
are the same.

The word *befriending* has been adopted to describe what
Samaritans do. Sally Casper, Co-Director of the Samaritans of
Boston, USA, put it succinctly. Writing in *Answers to Suicide*,[168]
she described the essential nature of befriending as: 'to respond
to a suicidal person as a friend, on an equal level, and treat him

or her exactly as we ourselves would want to be treated — with unconditional, uncritical acceptance and respect'. It is, she says, a therapeutic, not a social, relationship. What, one might ask, is the difference? One obvious distinguishing feature is that, whereas in social relationships we discriminate between those whom we wish to have as our friends and those we do not, there is no such discrimination in Samaritan befriending. Acceptance and respect are unconditionally bestowed on all who seek help. Thus, whatever cause a caller may feel he has to be ashamed, however much he or his deeds may meet with and warrant the disapproval of society, he will be befriended. This is not to say that those who befriend in any way condone, assent to or co-operate in grossly antisocial behaviour but it is accepted that despair and suicidal feelings can afflict *all* kinds of human beings. If we see someone drowning we do not ask what sort of person he is before deciding to throw him a lifebelt. A second aspect of Samaritan befriending which distinguishes it from purely social relationships is that there is an imbalance of constraints. The caller is free to make and break contact as he wishes. He can terminate a telephone conversation merely by replacing the receiver. He can walk out of a Samaritan centre and take his own life. His relationship with his befriender imposes no obligations upon him. The Samaritan on the other hand is bound by the rules of his organization and is not free to pursue self-interest in his relationship with the caller.

Many callers make more than one approach to the Samaritans. Throughout a period of crisis they may have regular and frequent conversations. When it seems to be relevant to the caller's plight the Samaritans may offer longer-term befriending, possibly allocating it to one or a small number of their volunteers. It is important that such arrangements do not as a matter of course go on indefinitely. Their purpose is to support the caller through a difficult period in his life and their objective is to enable him to return to the state where he no longer feels he needs to be supported. It is no part of the Samaritans' role to create dependence.

The Samaritans are there to be approached and, whilst they have to create a general awareness of their existence, they do not seek out their clients. They offer help to those who request it but they do not intrude into the life of anyone. There is, however, one type of call which may on occasion lead to more positive action. This is where someone approaches the Samaritans with anxiety about the welfare of another person. The Samaritans' immediate concern is to befriend the caller so troubled. If they are satisfied, however, that the third person is despairing, depressed or suicidal they may discreetly offer befriending. It is as a result of such approaches that the Samaritans have been able to help those too depressed to make the initial contact themselves. If it is clear, however, that the offer of befriending is unwelcome, the Samaritans will withdraw immediately. The decision to do so is a necessary consequence of the third principle, which affirms the autonomy of the individual:

A caller does not lose the freedom to make his own decisions, including the decision to take his own life, and is free to break contact at any time.

Looked at from any point of view this makes sense. If we consider it merely as a matter of what is practical it becomes clear that without the power to apply constant physical restraint the Samaritan is not going to be able to prevent a caller from taking his own life if that is what he really wants to do. Conceivably it might be possible to thwart a particular suicide attempt, but there is always another opportunity. As for the freedom to break contact at any time, it is self-evident: the caller can put down the receiver or walk out of the Samaritan centre if and when it pleases him to do so. From the ethical standpoint the third principle is nothing more or less than a statement of the individual's right to self-determination. As has already been indicated, however, our concern to uphold this right can be at odds with our natural instinct to preserve life. The Samaritan in telephone contact with an anonymous caller who has taken an overdose and who resolutely refuses to accept medical assistance is powerless. But what does he do when he is in the presence of someone who says: 'I want you to stay with me until I die'? The principle has to be observed and yet the Samaritan cannot sit by and let death occur. So long as the caller remains conscious his right to self-determination prevails, but as soon as he falls into unconsciousness responsibility for him passes to the Samaritan, who must then swiftly seek medical help. This being so, the Samaritan must warn the caller of his intention at an early stage. In practice the caller often accedes to the suggestion that an ambulance be called. Often too there is a weakening of the resolve to go through with the suicidal act as the overdose begins to take effect.

Quite apart from the practical and ethical standpoints there is in the context of the third principle a whole area which, for want of a better word, I shall label efficacy. To be effective in helping the suicidal, Samaritans have to be able to develop a befriending relationship. Like any other human relationship this has to be based on trust and mutual respect. Principle number three is thus *a sine qua non*. The caller can trust the Samaritan only if he knows his independence is not going to be compromised. This does not mean, of course, that the Samaritan should not seek the permission of the caller to stay with him throughout a period of crisis, but if the request is refused the Samaritan must allow the caller to go his own way. It can be a heavy price to pay for the possibility of being able to help. When a caller exercises his right and terminates his call with the real or apparent intention of suicide the Samaritan is likely to feel a sense of failure. 'Did I let the caller down?' 'Was there something I might have said that would have encouraged him to persevere?' It is at such moments that the Samaritan has need of the support that his colleagues can give him. Painful though it may at times be, the Samaritan has to remember that he could not help his callers without the trust and respect the third principle demands of him.

Trust and respect for those who are being counselled demand also that total confidentiality be observed. This is the basis of the fourth of the seven principles:

> *The fact that a person has asked the help of the Samaritans, together with everything he has said, is completely confidential within the organisation unless permission is freely given by the caller for all or a part of such information to be communicated to someone outside the organisation. A Samaritan volunteer is not permitted to accept confidences if a condition is made that not even the Director should be informed of them.*

It is self-evident that what has been disclosed to a Samaritan in a trusting relationship *must* be treated as absolutely confidential. Being a Samaritan places a most rigid demand on the volunteer not to reveal to *anyone* outside the organization any information about a caller, including the fact that someone has been or is a caller. Only if requested to or if given very clear permission to pass information outside the organization may the Samaritan do so, and then only to those persons specified by the caller. It is the secrecy of the confessional. The stricture against accepting confidences that are to be withheld from the Director of the Samaritan Branch is necessary if volunteers are to be able to function effectively with the support they need. Although a close relationship may be formed between a caller and an individual volunteer it is the Samaritan organization which helps the caller. No caller need be dependent upon just one Samaritan. All are there to help if need be. Moreover it is important that the individual Samaritan volunteer is not left isolated with the burden of a particular caller's distress. Such burdens have to be shared, and the Samaritan organization has been designed to provide the support that volunteers must have. This will be referred to again when we look at the fifth principle.

Occasionally situations arise in which, to the individual volunteer, it appears that there is a conflict between his vow of confidentiality and his duty as a citizen. If, for example, he hears what sounds like evidence of a crime having been committed he may feel that it would be in society's interest that he passed the information on to an outside body. This he cannot do and it is in such instances that he must tell his Branch Director, with whom the responsibility rests. The Director, of course, is bound by the same inviolable rule of confidentiality. Instances of the kind referred to are rare and when they do occur it is worth stopping to think about the possible reason for the individual concerned having called the Samaritans. In all probability, if his story is true (and by no means all such stories *are* true — some callers have a need to fantasize), he has called because he is distressed and the Samaritans can help him, and ultimately society, by encouraging him to think through the case for owning up to the crime. It must be remembered too that the majority of calls received by the Samaritans are anonymous. Callers are free to withhold their names and for many the ability to do so makes it easier for them to talk uninhibitedly. Even although for the purpose of conversation a first name has been used there is no reason why it should be the caller's real one.

Anonymity is the right of the caller. It is also the right of the Samaritan volunteer and consequently Samaritans are normally known only by a first name and often by a number. This has three advantages. First, it protects the privacy of the volunteer, preventing his Samaritan activities from intruding into his home life and that of his family. Secondly, the fact that the Samaritan, like the caller, is an anonymous person may make intimate discussion easier. Thirdly, Samaritans feel that potential callers may be discouraged from making contact if they are aware that an acquaintance is a member of the branch concerned. Useful as the anonymity of the Samaritans is, it has the disadvantage that the public at large might perceive the organization as having a somewhat faceless quality. This would be unfortunate, for it is important that Samaritans are known to be what they are: ordinary people who have no authority and whose ability to be of service to the suicidal and despairing depends solely upon their willingness to befriend. So some compromise is necessary, and many Samaritans make limited appearances in public, often in areas other than those in which they serve.

Ordinary people though they are, Samaritans are selected and given preparation for their work. Not everyone who would like to be a volunteer is suitable. Some people offer their services because they have been through some kind of traumatic experience and feel they would like to help others similarly afflicted. This is a worthy reason for wishing to be a Samaritan, but it has to be established that the person concerned has truly recovered from his unhappy experience and will be able to cope with the emotional stress of hearing others speaking of their similar plights. It must be clear, too, that the person who *has* recovered does not believe that he has a way of coping which would be suitable for all Samaritan callers. Many well-meaning and most effective members of society have a strong desire to solve other people's problems for them. Their talents would be better used elsewhere. They would probably find it frustrating to confine their activities to non-directive counselling. And the suicidal and despairing, plagued as they often are by feelings of inadequacy, might find it hard to believe that such people, whose own lives seem to be so efficiently run, could possibly understand them. Some potential volunteers are unsuitable because their commendable and sincerely held beliefs might make it impossible for them to adopt a neutral stance when talking to callers. They might feel, for example, that their consciences would not allow them to withhold advice against abortion, when what the girl with an unwanted pregnancy in fact needs above all is help to sort out her *own* thoughts on the matter.

Those volunteers who are selected have to undergo some preparation. The purpose of this is to give them an understanding of how the Samaritans work and a feel for the kinds of calls they will be likely to receive. Above all, the preparation classes are aimed at helping the volunteer to develop his listening skills, to enable him to focus his attention on the caller and his feelings, in other words to adopt a client-centred approach. Training is an unending activity. Samaritans find that they learn from experience and that this learning process never ends. The person who 'knows it all' is no Samaritan. No volunteer can 'go it alone'; *all* Samaritans need support, and the fifth principle recognizes this: —

> *Samaritan volunteers in befriending callers will be guided and actively supported by experienced leaders who will have the advice, when required, of professional consultants.*

It is a friendly and supportive organization, but it is a highly disciplined one. The Branch Director, whose appointment is made at a national level, has full authority. This is necessary not least because it may from time to time be desirabe to control the level of involvement of a particular volunteer with a caller. Perhaps the volunteer's concern for the caller's distress has reached the stage where it would be in the interests of both parties that other volunteers became involved. Decisions of this kind can be very difficult for the individual volunteer to take for himself and only the total authority of the Director is effective. The Director and his team of leaders have as their prime objective the welfare of the callers, but they also have responsibility for the performance and well-being of the volunteers. The volunteer is working at the sharp end. It is he who is in direct contact with the distressed caller. It is his emotional strength that is being drained. He needs the support of colleagues, especially those who, at that moment, are not immediately involved. They provide the still centre to which the volunteer can return.

There are times when it is necessary to seek professional advice. It may be, for example, that a caller is in very frequent and regular contact with the Branch and there is a concern that he might have some psychiatric problem which is not being helped by the service the Organization offers. It is then of great value for the Samaritans to have access to professional advice. Often a few minutes' discussion (without, of course, revealing the identity of the caller) with a psychologist or psychiatrist is all that is needed. Usually the advice given is to befriend in the normal way, but occasionally the Samaritan is told that he is probably dealing with a psychopathic person who is beyond the kind of help he can offer and it then becomes necessary to place some restriction on the frequency and duration of calls. Sometimes it is suggested that the caller should be asked for permission to refer his case to a professional therapist. Thus the sixth principle states:

> *In appropriate cases the caller will also be invited to consider
> seeking professional help in such fields as medicine and social
> work, and material help from other agencies.*

Thus if it appears that the caller is suffering from endogenous
depression the Samaritan will ask him to consider the possibility
of seeking medical assistance. Some callers, too, have very real
practical problems for which material help is necessary and once
again the Samaritan would ask the caller to consider, for example,
an approach to a solicitor or an accommodation agency. This is
quite correctly regarded as referral, but it does not mean that the
caller is merely being passed on to another agency. While, and
possibly after, his material and medical problems are being dealt
with the caller is still likely to be under stress and in need of the
kind of help the Samaritans offer. This will be given.

Many people, perhaps understandably, think that the Samaritan
organization is a religious one. The name, with its origin in the
biblical parable of the Good Samaritan, certainly seems to support
the notion. There is, however, no truth in it. Many volunteers
are in fact practising Christians, but a great many belong to other
faiths or to none. The organization recruits its members from all
walks of life, regardless of their views or persuasions, the only
stipulation in this context being that they do not attempt to impart
their opinions to the caller. The seventh principle is quite clear
on this issue:

> *Samaritan volunteers are forbidden to impose their own
> convictions or to influence callers in regard to politics, philosophy
> or religion.*

It is a natural human failing to assume that what we have found
to be beautiful, true and helpful will be regarded in the same way
by others. In fact the lines of poetry or the music that move me
more often than not have no such effect upon others, and it would
be arrogant and insensitive of me to think it ought to be otherwise.
It is insulting and in the end futile to attempt to do any of the
things forbidden in the seventh principle, insulting because we
should be implying that we knew better than the caller, and futile
because he can start only from where *he* is, not from where we
are. The Samaritan is not there because of his wisdom or
knowledge. He is not there to instruct or to advise. He is there
to befriend, to emphathize.

So much for the Samaritans themselves; let us conclude with

a brief look at their callers. Who are they? The answer is everyman. Suicide and feelings of despair are not confined to any class or sex. Callers come from all walks of life, from the employed and those who have no work, from the rich and the poor, from the clever and the not so clever, from those who have benefited from advanced education and those who have had little or even none, from those who live alone to those who are members of large families or who live in institutions, from those with homes in the city to those who live in isolated spots and those who have no homes at all. There is no group which does not or has not at some time furnished callers. Relatively few come from the immigrant population, perhaps because they have their own support systems or because they do not like to look for help. Fewer than might be expected come from the elderly, perhaps because they are not accustomed to the idea of going to others for help or perhaps because they do not like using the telephone. But more than might be expected come from the young, even the very young. The problems they bring to the Samaritans are most frequently to do with difficulties in their relationships with parents or teachers. They, like all other callers, need someone who will listen sympathetically and help them, give them time to sort out their own thoughts. Some callers, often younger ones, make 'testing' calls, perhaps trying to find out what kind of response they will get. Some make abusive calls — who else can they sound off to if no one ever gives them an ear? Some callers want the volunteers to talk about themselves, which is not what the Samaritans are there for and somehow or other it becomes necessary for the volunteer to ensure that it is the caller who talks about his own concerns and anxieties. Some callers telephone but cannot bring themselves to speak at all and, faced with a silent call, the volunteer has to wait patiently and encourage the caller to overcome whatever prevents him from speaking. Whoever the caller is, the Samaritan offers him uncritical acceptance and respect, enabling him to speak of things he may never have uttered before, things that occupy in his mind that dark and dangerous territory between life and death. It is a humbling task but it can be a rewarding one. There may be no thanks — none is expected — but there is an offer of hope, a lifeline.

12.

FURTHER READING

How many a man has dated a new era in his life from the reading
of a book!

Henry David Thoreau, *Walden*

Serendipity is an excellent guide to reading if what we seek is
pleasure and the satisfaction of passing curiosity. But when a
subject interests us or a book, such as this one, raises as many
questions in the reader's mind as it answers a more structured
approach may be desirable. Having said that I would add that
it is not my intention to recommend a course of reading on suicide.
It is perhaps necessary that there are among us those who give
serious thought to the study of such aspects of human behaviour
— we need thanatologists just as we need obstetricians — but
the spirit should have more than an undiluted diet of books on
the darker side of life. (That is why I felt it desirable to include
in Chapter 3 as a kind of counterbalance the life-affirming thoughts
expressed in Hemingway's *Old Man and the Sea.*[62]) With this
proviso — call it a 'health warning' if you must — I should like
to suggest a few books you might find interesting and informative.
Several of them are out of print but all can be obtained through
local libraries thanks to their excellent Interloans service.

No serious study of suicide would be complete without
reference to the books of Durkheim and Halbwachs. Durkheim's
Suicide[6] is a classic. Subtitled *A Study in Sociology*, it offers
valuable reading to the student of sociology as well as to those
interested in its main theme. It represents an important landmark
in the development of social science. As George Simpson, the
Editor of the first edition in English, said in his preface, it 'remains
the prototype of systematic, rigorous and unrelenting attack on
the subject with the data, techniques and accumulated knowledge

available at any given period'. It was 'among the very first modern examples of consistent and organized use of statistical method in social investigation'. Although one would probably not wholly subscribe to the conclusions he reached, Durkheim's book is well worth reading, not least for the description it gives of the three categories of suicide he defined (egoistic, altruistic and anomic). Halbwachs' book, *The Causes of Suicide*,[7] should be read after Durkheim's, for the study it describes is a continuation of the latter's work. Halbwachs' chief contribution was to show that the explanations of suicide, the social and the psychopathological, which his predecessor had regarded as being in conflict with each other, were in fact complementary.

Among the more recent books on suicide Professor Erwin Stengel's *Suicide and Attempted Suicide*[68] deals in a scholarly way with various aspects of the subject, including the statistics, motives and causes, the relevance of mental disorders, the attitude of society and prevention. A psychiatrist with extensive experience of research on suicide and attempted suicide, Professor Stengel was President of the International Association for Suicide Prevention. His book, first published in 1964, is a useful account of the facts of and theories concerning suicide. Its treatment of the statistics is lucid and interesting. For those who wish to focus on this aspect a booklet, *Suicide and Deliberate Self-Harm*,[166] produced by the Office of Health Economics may be of interest, as also should the papers published by the Office of Population Censuses and Surveys.[10, 11] The statistics of suicide in the United States are discussed in Corrine Loing Hatton and Sharon McBride Valente's book, *Suicide Assessment and Intervention*.[169] The chief virtue of this book, however, is that it deals in a readable way with the counselling of the potentially suicidal and those who have been bereaved through suicide. David K. Reynolds and Norman Farberow have written a fascinating account of the suicidal patient in the environment of the psychiatric hospital. Aptly entitled *Suicide Inside and Out*,[170] it includes the day-to-day notes written by one of the authors during a two-week period he spent as a patient, having got himself admitted as a severely depressed, suicidal veteran. The work of the Samaritans is the subject of three books, two of them edited by Chad Varah (*The Samaritans: Befriending the Suicidal*,[171] and *The Samaritans in the '80s*[172]) and the third (*Answers to Suicide*[173]) presented to him by the Samaritans on the occasion of the twenty-fifth anniversary of their founding. All three feature contributions by several people with long experience of Samaritan work.

The books of Professor Edwin Shneidman are well worth seeking out. One, *Essays in Self-Destruction*,[155] is a compilation of several essays by various authors including Shneidman himself. The variety of subjects makes this a fascinating book. These range from 'Dead to the World: The Passions of Herman Melville' and 'Shakespeare's Suicides: Some Historic, Dramatic and Psychological Reflections' to 'The Components of Personal Despair' and 'The Psychology of the Fatal Accident'. There is also an essay, 'Can a Mouse Commit Suicide?', which concludes on an agnostic note. Another of Shneidman's books, *Voices of Death*,[63] contains a series of personal documents from people facing death. It is a beautiful and poignant book. It is also very moving. Once, when I was on the telephone a friend who had dropped in to see me spotted my copy lying on my desk and began to browse through it. Moments later, when I had completed my telephone call I turned round to find her in tears. It is *not* light reading.

For those who are interested in the historical and literary side of suicide there are two notable books, One, long out of print, is Henry Romilly Fedden's *Suicide, A Social and Historical Study*[13] which contains a wealth of references to the literature of suicide, from classical to more recent times. The other is *The Savage God*[71] by the poet and critic, A. Alvarez. It begins with a prologue in which Alvarez presents a moving account of the life and death of the young American poetess, Sylvia Plath, who took her own life in 1963. He also speaks of his own unsuccessful attempted suicide. The rest of this beautifully written book deals with both the cultural and theoretical aspects of suicide and a most illuminating account from the perspective of literature.

Mention of Sylvia Plath brings us to the subject of works of fiction. Her novel, *The Bell Jar*,[43] is the story of an American girl's breakdown, her attempted suicide and the treatment she receives. It is only one of many novels from which much can be learned of the inner experience of the suicidal. Two others have been much quoted in the present book: Flaubert's *Madame Bovary*[36] and Tolstoy's *Anna Karenina*.[18] The latter is undoubtedly in a class of its own and has few rivals as a piece of literature. If not *the* greatest novel in any language, it is certainly one of those that would appear on most lists of the top ten. Quite apart from its stature as a work of art and the desirability of reading it for its vivid panoramic view of Russian life it is worth reading or re-

reading for the insights it offers on the state of mind of the suicidal.

There are, of course, many books which one might recommend for further information on some of the subsidiary subjects dealt with in the present volume. Much has been written on depression. Not least of these is Dr Caroline Shreeve's book, *Depression — Its Causes and How to Overcome It*,[81] which is another member of the present series of Life Crisis Books. Other books, which like Dr Shreeve's give an account of depressive illness and how it can be dealt with, include Dr Andrew Stanway's *Overcoming Depression*[69] and Jack Dominion's *Depression*.[174] John White's *The Masks of Melancholy*[76] considers depression and suicide from the viewpoint of a Christian psychiatrist. Dorothy Rowe's *Depression — The Way Out of Your Prison*[78] presents a somewhat different approach to those offered in many other books. She describes how the depressed live in a prison they have built for themselves and how they resist all attempts to get them to leave it. She treats depression as a moral issue and she suggests an approach which many might find helpful in securing release from their self-imprisonment.

Finally, mention should be made of two of Dr Tony Lake's books: *Living With Grief*[84] and *Loneliness*.[35] The first of these is a helpful account of bereavement, which takes a positive view of the grieving process. It makes special reference to bereavement through suicide. The second is a sensitive attempt to help those who are lonely. It might prove useful to some of those who are beginning to feel a sense of isolation, which is after all with depression one of the precursors of suicide.

POSTSCRIPT

The only end of writing is to enable the readers better to enjoy
life or better to endure it.

Samuel Johnson, review of Soames Jenyns,
The Enquiry into the Nature and Origin of Evil

In his book, *Ninety-Nine Novels*,[175] Anthony Burgess says that
'a novel ought to leave in the reader's mind a sort of philosophical
residue'. Can it be that a work of non-fiction should do so too?
What sort of philosophical residue does one expect from a book
on suicide? Can reading such a book enable the reader better
to enjoy life or better to endure it? One can only hope that by
helping to make suicide more comprehensible those who feel
suicidal might be encouraged to seek help and those who are
confronted by the suicidal thoughts of others might feel better
able to provide it. I have tried not to moralize about suicide. After
all, one does not help the suicidal by telling them that what they
are contemplating is wrong. And yet I *do* have a view. It may
be of little value to anyone but myself, yet I owe it to myself and
possibly to the reader to say what it is.

I am not a Christian; nor am I an atheist. So I do not feel strongly
about sin; nor do I wish to argue with those who do. It does
not seem to me that suicide is intrinsically wrong, though I think
it can be an act of beastly cruelty to those who have to live with
the consequences. Neither do I think that suicide is ever
intrinsically right, though I have a great deal of sympathy with
those whose circumstances have brought them to the awful
conclusion that it is the *only* course left to them. I find no profit
to think in terms of courage or cowardice. Suicide can be either:
for me it would take more courage than I have; for my neighbour
whose courage is not enough to enable him to face tomorrow

it requires little. But although suicide may be neither wrong nor cowardly and though I believe that we have the right to dispose of our own lives as we see fit, I am opposed to it.

I am not absolutely certain what lies behind my aversion to suicide. Perhaps it is the feeling that to kill oneself is to waste life. I recoil from all wastage of this unique awareness, this irreplaceable potentiality, whether it is unintended death through accident or wanton killing, as in war, but especially when it is the consequence of a deliberate act of self-destruction. Perhaps my abhorrence of suicide is the result of some long-forgotten indoctrination which I shall never fathom. Perhaps it lies in some subconscious taboo. Undoubtedly it is sustained by the joy of being alive:

> There's night and day, brother, both sweet things; sun, moon and stars, brother, all sweet things; there's likewise a wind on the heath. Life is very sweet, brother; who would wish to die?[176]

I cannot rationalize it even to my own satisfaction. I feel that, in some strange way and for reasons which are inaccessible to me, *suicide ought not to be possible*. How can consciousness put an end to itself? How can a free act terminate the freedom which made it possible? It is as though a candle were to extinguish itself because it could not tolerate the brilliance of its own light. Perhaps this paradox which prevents my acceptance of suicide is the very reason that drives others to it: life can no longer bear itself. There *has* to be an alternative.

APPENDIX

Table 1*

Suicides per Year per 100,000 of Population

Country	1841-5	1881-5	1901-5	1911-13	1914-18	1919-22
Australia	—	10	13	13	12	11
Austria	5	17	17	20	22	24
Belgium	6	11	12	14	—	13
Denmark	23	25	23	18	18	14
England and Wales	—	8	10	10	9	10
Finland	4	4	6	10	9	10
France	9	19	23	25	18	22
Germany	—	21	21	22	17	21
Holland	—	5	6	6	6	6
Hungary	—	8	18	19	15	26
Ireland	—	2	3	4	—	3
Italy	—	5	6	8	8	8
Japan	—	15	20	19	19	19
New Zealand	—	—	15	13	12	12
Norway	11	7	6	6	4	5
Scotland	—	5	6	6	5	5
Spain	—	3	2	5	6	5
Sweden	7	10	14	18	13	14
Switzerland	—	23	23	24	21	21
United States	—	—	14	16	15	12

* Figures are based on data quoted by Halbwachs in *Les Causes du Suicide*,[7] which were derived from Handwörterbuch der Staatswissenschaften, 4th edition, 1925.

Table 2*

Suicides per 100,000 of Population

Country	Year	Male	Female	All
Hungary	1977	56	26	40
Germany (GDR)	1974	46	28	36
Finland	1975	41	10	25
Denmark	1977	31	18	24
Austria	1977	35	15	24
Switzerland	1977	34	14	24
Germany (FED)	1977	30	16	23
Czechoslovakia	1975	33	12	22
Sweden	1977	28	11	20
Japan	1977	22	14	18
Belgium	1976	22	11	17
France	1976	23	9	16
Bulgaria	1977	21	8	14
United States	1976	19	7	13
Canada	1975	18	7	12
Poland	1976	21	4	12
Norway	1977	17	6	11
Australia	1977	16	6	11
Iceland	1977	17	4	10
New Zealand	1976	13	6	9
Holland	1977	12	7	9
England and Wales	1978	10	6	8
Scotland	1977	10	7	8
Israel	1977	8	5	7
Northern Ireland	1977	5	4	5
Spain	1975	6	2	4
Greece	1976	4	2	3

* Figures are based on WHO statistics published in *Suicide and Deliberate Self-Harm*. Office of Health Economics, 1981.[166]
Note: The figures for 'Male' refer to the number of males per 100,000 of the male population of the country who committed suicide; the figures for 'Female' to the number of females per 100,000 of the female population who committed suicide; and the figures for 'All' to the number of people per 100,000 of the total population who committed suicide.

Table 3*

Deaths from Suicide in England and Wales by Sex and Age in 1983

Age	Men Suicides	Percentage	Women Suicides	Percentage	All Suicides	Percentage
10-14	2	0.0	6	0.4	8	0.1
15-19	84	3.0	24	1.6	108	2.5
20-24	191	6.8	65	4.4	256	6.0
25-29	223	7.9	55	3.7	278	6.5
30-34	257	9.1	61	4.2	318	7.4
35-39	281	10.0	110	7.5	391	9.1
40-44	242	8.6	93	6.3	335	7.8
45-49	226	8.0	116	7.9	342	8.0
50-54	250	8.9	134	9.1	384	9.0
55-59	246	8.7	152	10.4	398	9.3
60-64	243	8.6	159	10.8	402	9.4
65-69	187	6.7	136	9.3	323	7.5
71-74	152	5.4	151	10.3	303	7.1
75-79	129	4.6	101	6.9	230	5.4
80-84	73	2.6	60	4.1	133	3.1
85 +	26	0.9	44	3.0	70	1.6
	2,812		1,467		4,279	

* Based on figures provided by the Office of Population Censuses and Surveys.

Table 4*

Suicide Rates for Urban and Rural Areas
Suicides per 100,000

	Men 1959-63	1970-2	Women 1959-63	1970-72
Conurbations	15.7	10.3	10.7	7.6
Urban areas				
100,000 +	14.5	9.9	9.9	6.5
50,000-100,000	14.0	9.0	10.4	7.5
Under 50,000	13.6	8.3	8.6	5.7
Rural areas	11.8	9.4	6.4	5.3
England and Wales	14.1	9.5	9.3	6.5

* Figures based upon *Suicides 1961-74*, published by the Office of Population Censuses and Surveys.[10]

Table 5*

Suicide Methods in 1980
Percentages for England and Wales

	Men	Women
Poisoning by liquid and solid substances	24.8	54.3
Domestic gas	0.4	0.0
Other gas	16.6	2.7
Hanging, strangulation and suffocation	29.3	17.2
Drowning	5.4	12.1
Firearms	8.1	0.4
Cutting and piercing instruments	2.7	1.8
Jumping from high places	4.3	4.9

* Figures taken from *Suicides 1950-82*, published by the Office of Population Censuses and Surveys.[11]

Table 6*

Lethality Scoring

The left side of the table deals with thoughts of suicide and the plan the individual may have for its execution. Choose the one description from the list which is most appropriate and record the number of points allocated to it. Then to this number add the points for all the relevant items on the right-hand list.

Imminent sudden death	8 points	Previous suicidal acts	up to 4
Imminent slow method suicide	7 "	Absence of hope	3
Planning sudden death	6 "	Loss of faith	3
Planning slow method suicide	5 "	Recent broken relationship	3
Planning a suicide gamble	4 "	Isolation	3
Planning a suicide gesture	3 "	Rejection	3
Definite suicide thoughts, no plan	2 "	Depressive illness (endogenous)	2
Vague thoughts of suicide	1 "	Dependence on alcohol or	
No suicidal thoughts	0 "	drugs	2
		Possession of means of suicide	2
		Putting affairs in order	2
		Over 60 years of age	1
		Male	1
		Illness	1
		Chronic pain	1

A total score of 20 suggests that the person is in imminent danger and should not be left alone.
A score of 14 or over indicates the need for a further contact very soon.
A score of 6 or more indicates the desirability of further contact but with less urgency.

* Based on Roy Vining's *Assessing Suicide Risk* in Chad Varah's *The Samaritans: Befriending the Suicidal.*[170]

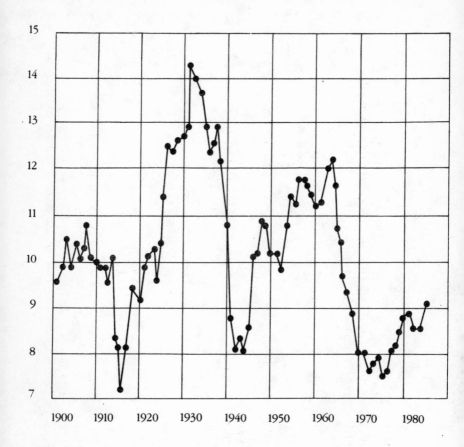

Diagram 1.

Suicide Rate in England and Wales, 1901-84, deaths per 100,000.
Based upon figures from the Office of Population
Censuses and Surveys

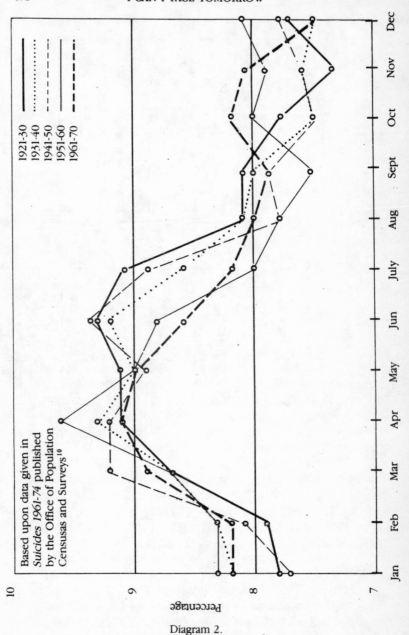

Diagram 2.

Percentage distribution of suicides by month of occurrence, 1921-70
in England and Wales. Each month's figures are corrected to a thirty-day month.

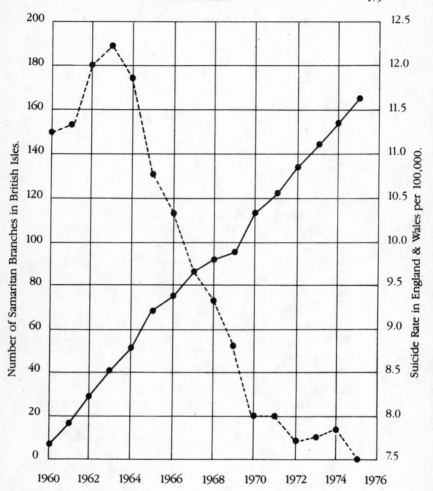

Diagram 3.

Based on data given in Chart Variations. The Samaritans: Befriending
the Suicidal[170]

Suicide Rate ----------
Number of Samaritan Branches _____

REFERENCES

1. Richard Cobb, *Death in Paris, 1795-1801*, quoted in *The Oxford Book of Death* (Oxford University Press, 1983).
2. Albert Camus, *The Myth of Sisyphus*, translated by Justin O'Brien (Vintage Books, 1955).
3. Werner Heisenberg, *Physics and Philosophy* (Allen & Unwin, 1963).
4. Frank Muir, *The Frank Muir Book* (Heinemann, 1976).
5. The *Guardian*, 4 November 1985.
6. Emile Durkheim, *Suicide — A Study in Sociology*, translated by John A. Spaulding and George Simpson (Routledge & Kegan Paul, 1970).
7. Maurice Halbwachs, *The Causes of Suicide*, translated by Harold Goldblatt (Routledge & Kegan Paul, 1978).
8. Kreitman, N., and Philip, A. E., *Parasuicide*, Brit. J. Psychiat. 1969, *115*, 746-7.
9. Quoted by Kreitman, N., *Parasuicide* (John Wiley, 1977).
10. Adelstein, A., and Mardon, C., *Suicides 1961-74*, Office of Population Censuses and Surveys Population Trends 2, Winter 1975 (Government Statistical Service).
11. Bulusu, L., and Alderson, M., *Suicides 1950-82*, Office of Population Censuses and Surveys Population Trends 35, Spring 1984 (Government Statistical Service).
12. Nancy Allen in *Suicide Assessment and Intervention*, edited by Corrine Loing Hatton and Sharon McBride Valente (Appleton-Century-Crofts, 1984).
13. Henry Romilly Fedden, *Suicide — A Social and Historical Study* (Peter Davies Ltd, 1938).
14. Charles Caleb Colton, *Lacon*, quoted in *The International Thesaurus of Quotations* (Penguin Books Ltd, 1983).
15. Sigmund Freud, *Beyond the Pleasure Principle*, quoted in Reference 13.

16. Eric Berne, *A Layman's Guide to Psychiatry and Psychoanalysis* (Penguin Books, 1978).
17. Miguel de Cervantes, *Don Quixote*, quoted in *The International Thesaurus of Quotations* (Penguin Books, 1983).
18. Leo Tolstoy, *Anna Karenina*, translated by Rosemary Edmonds (the Folio Society, 1975).
19. C. S. Lewis, quoted by John Wain in *The Living World of Shakespeare* (Penguin Books, 1966).
20. William Cowper, *The Needless Alarm, A Choice of Cowper's Verse* selected by Norman Nicholson (Faber & Faber, 1975).
21. Voltaire, 'Cato', *Philosophical Dictionary*, quoted in *The International Thesaurus of Quotations* (Penguin Books, 1983).
22. Anthony Newley and Leslie Bricusse, Title of Musical.
23. Alfred, Lord Tennyson, *The Two Voices*, Poetical Works (Oxford University Press, 1953).
24. Sigmund Freud, *Thoughts for the Times on War and Death*, quoted in *The Oxford Book of Death* (Oxford University Press, 1983).
25. John Keats, *Ode to a Nightingale* The New Oxford Book of English Verse (Oxford University Press, 1972).
26. Robert Graves, *Poems Selected by Himself* (Penguin Books, 1972).
27. Henry Purcell's opera, *Dido and Aeneas*, text by Nahum Tate.
28. Anna Akhmatova, *Selected Poems* (Penguin Books, 1969).
29. James Thomson ('B.V.'), *The City of Dreadful Night* (Reeves & Turner and Bertram Dobell, 1888, Ballantyne Press).
30. Irving Berent, *The Algebra of Suicide* (Human Sciences Press, 1981).
31. Fyodor Dostoevsky, *Crime and Punishment*, translated by Constance Garnett (Everyman's Library, J. M. Dent, 1958).
32. James C. Diggory, 'The Components of Personal Despair' in *Essays in Self-Destruction*, edited by Edwin S. Shneidman (Science House, 1967).
33. Kresten Bjerg, *The Suicidal Life Space — Attempts at a Reconstruction from Suicide Notes*, in *Essays in Self-Destruction*, editd by Edwin S. Shneidman (Science House).
34. Albert Bayet, *Le Suicide et la Morale*, quoted in Reference 7.
35. Tony Lake, *Loneliness* (Sheldon Press, 1980).
36. Gustave Flaubert, *Madame Bovary*, translated by Alan Russell (Penguin Books, 1971).

37. John Jones, *Dostoevsky* (Oxford University Press, 1985).
38. Franz Kafka, *A Fasting Showman*, in *Wedding Preparations in the Country and Other Stories*, translated by Willa and Edwin Muir (Penguin Books, 1982).
39. Somerset Maugham, *The Narrow Corner*, quoted by W. Macneile Dixon in *The Human Situation* (Penguin Books, 1958).
40. William Mackepeace Thackeray, *Vanity Fair* (J.M.Dent,1924).
41. Harry Williams, *Some Day I'll Find You* (Mitchell Beazley International, 1983).
42. Johann Wolfgang von Goethe, *Die Leiden des jungen Werthers*, quoted in Reference 7.
43. Sylvia Plath, *The Bell Jar* (Faber & Faber, 1982).
44. *The Aeneid* of Virgil, translated by C. Day Lewis (Heron Books).
45. Arthur Miller, *After the Fall*, Collected Plays, Volume II (Martin Secker & Warburg, 1981).
46. Albert Camus, *The Outsider*, translated by Joseph Laredo (Penguin Books, 1984).
47. *The Sunday Times*, 24 February 1985.
48. Leo Tolstoy, *My Confession*, translated by 'Zonia', quoted by William James in *The Varieties of Religious Experience* (The Fontana Library, 1960).
49. Paul Webster and Nicholas Powell, *Saint-Germain-de Prés* (Constable, 1984).
50. Nadezhda Mandelstam, *Hope Against Hope*, translated by Max Hayward (Collins & Harvill Press, 1971).
51. Thomas Hardy, *Jude the Obscure* (Oxford University Press, 1985).
52. Fyodor Dostoevsky, *The Dream of a Queer Fellow* and the Pushkin Speech, translated by S. Kotelliansky and J. Middleton Murry (Unwin Books, 1972).
53. Alexander Solzhenitsyn, *The Gulag Archipelago* (Collins-Harvill and Fontana, 1974).
54. Evgenia S. Ginsburg, *Into the Whirlwind* (Penguin Books, 1968).
55. Viktor E. Frankl, *Man's Search for Meaning* (Hodder & Stoughton, 1982).
56. Fyodor Dostoevsky, *Notes from a Dead House*, translated by L. Navrozov and Y. Guralsky (Foreign Languages Publishing House, Moscow).
57. *The Literary Review*, February 1985.

58. W. Macneile Dixon, *The Human Situation* (Penguin Books, 1958).
59. Fyodor Dostoevsky, *The Brothers Karamazov*, translated by David Magarshack (Folio Books, 1965).
60. Professor A. Majocchi, *Life and Death*, quoted by W. Macneile Dixon in *The Human Situation* (Penguin Books, 1958).
61. Kern-Hammerstein II, from the musical, *Show Boat*.
62. Ernest Hemingway, *The Old Man and the Sea* (Jonathan Cape, 1958).
63. Edwin Shneidman, *Voices of Death* (Bantam Books, 1982).
64. Described by Eugene Kennedy in *Crisis Counselling* (Gill and Macmillan, 1981); see also Henry A. Murray's 'Dead to the World: The Passions of Herman Melville', in *Essays in Self-Destruction*, edited by Edwin S. Shneidman (Science House, 1967).
65. Carson McCullers, *The Heart is a Lonely Hunter* (Penguin Books, 1982).
66. J. P. Watson, *How Important is Imitation in Suicidal Acts?* in *Answers to Suicide* (Constable, 1978).
67. Presented at the Annual Conference of the Samaritans, York, 1984.
68. Erwin Stengel, *Suicide and Attempted Suicide* (Penguin Books, 1977).
69. Andrew Stanway, *Overcoming Depression* (Hamlyn Paperbacks, 1983).
70. Arthur Waley, *Chinese Poems* (George Allen & Unwin, 1961).
71. A. Alvarez, *The Savage God* (Penguin Books, 1974).
72. Sigmund Freud, quoted by 'Palinurus' (Cyril Vernon Connolly) in *The Unquiet Grave* (Penguin Books, 1967).
73. Bernie Zilbergeld, *The Shrinking of America* (Little, Brown and Company, 1983).
74. Thomas De Quincey, *The Confessions of an English Opium-Eater* (the Folio Society, 1963).
75. John Milton, *Samson Agonistes*, in *Poetry of the English-Speaking World*, edited by Richard Aldington (Readers' Union, 1950).
76. John White, *The Masks of Melancholy* (Inter-Varsity Press, 1983).
77. Bernard Rosenblum, *The Astrologer's Guide to Counselling* (CRCS Publications, 1983).
78. Dorothy Rowe, *Depression — The Way Out of Your Prison* (Routledge & Kegan Paul, 1984).

79. Edward J. Thomas, *The History of Buddhist Thought* (Routledge & Kegan Paul, 1971).
80. Anthony Storr, *The Integrity of the Personality* (Penguin Books, 1981).
81. Caroline Shreeve, *Depression — Its Causes and How to Overcome It* (Turnstone Press, 1984).
82. David Burns, *Feeling Good*, quoted by Bernie Zilbergeld in *The Shrinking of America* (Little, Brown & Co., 1983).
83. Lord Hailsham, *The Door Wherein I Went* (William Collins, 1975).
84. Tony Lake, *Living With Grief* (Sheldon Press, 1984).
85. *Chuang Tzu, Taoist Philosopher and Chinese Mystic*, translated by Herbert A. Giles (George Allen & Unwin, 1961).
86. William Shakespeare, *Julius Caesar*.
87. Francis Charles, *Hieroglyphics*, quoted in *The Oxford Dictionary of Quotations* (Oxford University Press, 1975).
88. Sir Edwin Arnold, *The Light of Asia* (Routledge & Kegan Paul, 1978).
89. Emily Dickinson, *The Bustle in a House, The Complete Poems of Emily Dickinson* (Faber & Faber, 1975).
90. Edward de Bono, *de Bono's Thinking Course* (BBC, 1982).
91. Keith Hawton and José Catalán, *Attempted Suicide* (Oxford University Press, 1982).
92. J. Bancroft and P. Marsack, *The Repetitiveness of Self-Poisoning and Self-Injury*, Brit. J. of Psychiat., 1977, *131*, 394-9.
93. R. A. Barnes, *Characteristics of the Chronic Suicide Attempter* (Proceedings Communication: 10th International Congress for Suicide Prevention and Crisis Intervention, Ottawa, 1979, 17-20).
94. E. S. Paykel, B. A. Prusoff and J. K. Myers, *Suicide Attempts and Recent Life Events: a Controlled Comparison*, Arch. of Gen. Psychiat., 1975, *32*, 327-33.
95. J. Bancroft, A. Skrimshire, J. Casson, O. Harvard-Watts and F. Reynolds, *People Who Deliberately Poison or Injure Themselves: Their Problems and Their Contacts with Helping Agencies*, Psychological Medicine, 1977, 7, 289-303.
96. J. Roberts and K. Hawton, *Child Abuse and Attempted Suicide*, Brit. J. of Psychiat., 1980, *137*, 319-23.
97. H. G. Morgan, C. J. Burns-Cox, H. Pocock and S. Pottle, *Deliberate Self-Harm: a Follow-Up Study of 279 Patients*, Brit. J. of Psychiat., 1975, *126*, 564-74.

98. T. Holding, D. Buglass, J. C. Duffy and N. Kreitman, *Parasuicide in Edinburgh — a Seven Year Review 1968-74*, Brit. J. of Psychiat., 1977, *130*, 534-43.

99. Steve Platt, *Unemployment and Parasuicide ('Attempted Suicide') in Edinburgh 1968-1982*, Unemployment Unit Bulletin, November 1983.

100. Michael R. Alderson, 'National Trends in Self-Poisoning in Women', *The Lancet*, April 1985, 974-5.

101. K. Hawton, J. O'Grady, M. Osborne and D. Cole, *Adolescents Who Take Overdoses: Their Characteristics, Problems and Contacts with Helping Agencies*, Brit. J. of Psychiat., 1982, *140*, 118-23.

102. Thomas Hardy, *Tess of the D'Urbervilles* (Penguin Books, 1985).

103. Josephus, *The Jewish War*, translated by G. A. Williamson (Penguin Books, 1985).

104. Napoleon, Order of the Day, quoted by Henry Romilly Fedden in *Suicide — A Social and Historical Study* (Peter Davies, 1938).

105. James Joyce, *Ulysses* (John Lane, Bodley Head, 1954).

106. *The Literary Review*, December 1984.

107. John Bayley in his review of *Feeling in Victorian Fiction* by Barbara Hardy, *The Literary Review*, March 1985.

108. Blaise Pascal, *The Pensées*, translated by J. M. Cohen (Penguin Books, 1961).

109. *Kobbé's Complete Opera Book*, edited by the Earl of Harewood (Putnam, 1954).

110. Richard Hoggart, *The Uses of Literacy* (Penguin Books, 1962).

111. R. T. Inoguchi, T. Nakajima and R. Pineau, *The Divine Wind: Japan's Kamikaze Force in World War II* (Hutchinson, 1959), quoted by John Hinton in *Dying* (Penguin Books, 1967).

112. Henry Scott Stokes, *The Life and Death of Yukio Mishima* (Penguin Books, 1985).

113. Seneca, *Letters from a Stoic*, translated by Robin Campbell (Penguin Books, 1982).

114. Epictetus, *The Discourses and Manual*, Vol. 1, translated by P. E. Matheson (Oxford University Press, 1938).

115. 'Palinurus' (Cyril Vernon Connolly), *The Unquiet Grave* (Penguin Books, 1967).

116. Friedrich Wilhelm Nietzsche, *Beyond Good and Evil*, translated by R. J. Hollingdale (Penguin Books, 1984).

117. Christiaan Barnard, *Good Life Good Death* (Peter Owen, 1985).

118. Alexander Chase, *Perspectives*, quoted in *The International Thesaurus of Quotations* (Penguin Books, 1983).

119. Sir John Betjeman, 'Churchyards', in *Church Poems* (John Murray, 1981).

120. Dorothy Parker, *Resumé*, quoted in *The International Thesaurus of Quotations* (Penguin Books, 1983).

121. Andrew Christie and Karen Heuler, *I Wasn't Kidding* (Angus & Robertson, 1984).

122. Richard Eberhart, *How It Is*, quoted in *The Penguin Dictionary of Modern Quotations* (Penguin Books, 1980).

123. *The Quran*, translated by Muhammad Zafrulla Khan (Curzon Press, 1981).

124. *Some Sayings of the Buddha*, translated by F. L. Woodward (the Buddhist Society by arrangement with Oxford University Press, 1973).

125. Heinrich Zimmer, *Philosophies of India* (Bollingen Foundation, 1953).

126. *Selected Writings of Mahatma Gandhi*, edited by Ronald Duncan (Faber & Faber, 1971).

127. *The Bhagavadgita*, translated by S. Radhakrishnan (George Allen & Unwin, 1960).

128. Judges 16:30.

129. 1 Sam. 30:4-5.

130. 2 Sam. 17:23.

131. 2 Macc. 14:37-46 (the Apocrypha).

132. St Augustine, *The City of God*, translated by Henry Bettenson (Penguin Books, 1986).

133. T. C. Kane, article on suicide in the *New Catholic Encyclopedia* (Catholic University of America, Washington D.C., 1967).

134. Graham Greene, *The Heart of the Matter* (Penguin Books, 1983).

135. G. K. Chesterton, *Orthodoxy* William Collins, Fontana Books, 1961).

136. Benedictus de Spinoza, *Ethics* (Heron Books, by arrangement with J. M. Dent).

137. T. H. Huxley, quoted by Henry Romilly Fedden in *Suicide — A Social and Historical Study* (Peter Davies, 1938).

138. Blackstone, quoted in *The Oxford English Dictionary*.

139. Aristotle, *Ethics*, translated by J. A. K. Thomson (Penguin Books, 1986).

140. Gustave Flaubert, *The Dictionary of Received Ideas* (Penguin Books, 1983).

141. Martial, *Epigrams*, quoted in *The International Thesaurus of Quotations* (Penguin Books, 1983).

142. Sir Thomas Browne, quoted by Henry Romilly Fedden in *Suicide — A Social and Historical Study* (Peter Davies, 1938).

143. Charles Caleb Colton in *Lacon*, quoted by Henry Romilly Fedden in *Suicide — A Social and Historical Study* (Peter Davies, 1938).

144. St Augustine, *The City of God*, paraphrased by Bertrand Russell in *A History of Western Philosophy* (George Allen & Unwin, 1947).

145. Plato, *The Trial and Execution of Socrates*, translated by Peter George (Folio Society, 1972).

146. Immanuel Kant, *The Metaphysic of Morality*, translated by John Watson in *Selections from Kant* (James Maclehose, 1908).

147. Ludwig Wittgenstein, *Notebooks 1914-1916* (Basil Blackwell, 1979).

148. Patrick Gardner, *Schopenhauer* (Penguin Books, 1963).

149. Marcus Aurelius, *Meditations*, translated by Maxwell Staniforth (Penguin Books, 1985).

150. John Donne, *Biathanatos*, in *John Donne — Selected Prose*, chosen by Evelyn Simpson, edited by Helen Gardner and Timothy Healy (Oxford University Press, 1967).

151. David Hume, *Of Suicide*, quoted by A. Alvarez in *The Savage God* (Penguin Books, 1974).

152. Fyodor Dostoevsky, *The Possessed*, translated by Constance Garnett (J. M. Dent, 1960).

153. Jean-Paul Sartre, *Between Existentialism and Marxism*, translated by John Matthews (Verso Editions, 1983).

154. Albert Camus, *The Rebel*, translated by Anthony Bower (Penguin Books, 1977).

155. *Essays in Self-Destruction*, edited by Erwin S. Shneidman (Science House, 1967).

156. Richard Dawkins, *The Selfish Gene* (Oxford University Press, 1976).

157. Eugène Marais, *The Soul of the White Ant* (Penguin Books, 1973).

158. Brian Clark, *Whose Life is it Anyway?*, title of play, 1972.

159. Report from General Practice 20: *Prevention of Psychiatric Disorders in General Practice* (Royal College of General Practitioners, 1981).

160. Quoted by Richard Nelson-Jones in *The Theory and Practice of Counselling Psychology* (Holt, Rinehart & Winston, 1982).
161. G. K. Chesterton, *The World State*, Collected Poems (Methuen, 1965).
162. Alexander Solzhenitsyn, *Cancer Ward* (Penguin Books, 1969).
163. Jean Racine, *Phaedra* (Penguin Books, 1984).
164. Publilius Syrus, *Moral Sayings*, quoted in *The International Thesaurus of Quotations* (Penguin Books, 1983).
165. Horace, *Ars Poetica*, quoted in *The Penguin International Thesaurus of Quotations* (Penguin Books, 1983).
166. *Suicide and Deliberate Self-Harm* (Office of Health Economics, 1981).
167. *Suicide — The Will to Live vs. The Will to Die*, edited by Norman Linzer (Human Science Press, 1984).
168. Sally Casper in *Answers to Suicide* (Constable, 1978).
169. *Suicide Assessment and Intervention*, edited by Corrine Loing Hatton and Sharon McBride Valente (Appleton-Century-Crofts, 1984).
170. David K. Reynolds and Norman L. Farberow, *Suicide: Inside and Out* (University of California Press, 1977).
171. Chad Varah, *The Samaritans: Befriending the Suicidal* (Constable, 1985).
172. Chad Varah, *The Samaritans in the '80s* (Constable, 1982).
173. *Answers to Suicide* presented to Chad Varah by the Samaritans on the 25th Anniversary of their Founding (Constable, 1978).
174. Jack Dominion, *Depression* (William Collins, 1984).
175. Anthony Burgess, *Ninety-nine Novels* (Allison & Busby, 1984).
176. George Borrow, *Lavengro* (J. M. Dent, 1924).

INDEX